How They Did It

How They Did It

Profiles of New Orleans Entrepreneurs

by Sally Forman
photography by Margaret Saer Beer

foreword by Emeril Lagasse

 Idea Village Press

ISBN 978-0-578-03114-9

Cover Photo "Cityscape at Night (2007)" by Richard Nowitz

Printed in Canada

The Idea Village

The Idea Village is a 501(c)(3) economic development organization founded in 2000 with the mission to identify, support and retain entrepreneurial talent in the New Orleans Region. Through 2009, The Idea Village has supported over 275 early-stage, high-impact New Orleans entrepreneurs by providing over 40,000 hours of business consulting and allocating over $2.5 million in capital to support their growth.

Idea Village Press
515 Girod Street
New Orleans, LA 70130
www.ideavillage.org

To entrepreneurs and those who believe in them.

CONTENTS

FOREWORD

Cooking is easy, but developing a business can be hard. There were times throughout the years as I was opening a new restaurant or growing my brand that I faced many challenges as an entrepreneur. I needed to expand my team, but that meant more capital, which often meant more products to develop and more hours in the kitchen.

Had it not been for my talented team, the focus and determination that I put into my work, and taking a few calculated risks, I wouldn't be where I am today.

Why did I succeed? I believe that most successful people have had mentors who helped them along the way. For me that was my mom, Hilda. She inspired my cooking from an early age, and she and my dad helped instill my strong work ethic. They also taught me to get up everyday and try a little harder than the day before. There were other entrepreneurs along the way who also inspired me – people like Ella Brennan and Julia Child. These captivating and driven people motivated me to succeed, and to become a better chef and restaurateur.

Along the way, I've tried to mentor young people and share my knowledge with them so they can succeed. I've also tried to help other chefs and restaurateurs develop and grow their businesses. I've shared the knowledge and wisdom that I've learned in the hopes that they can experience the success that I've enjoyed, and pass it on to the next generation. I believe that the more you give back, the more you get in return.

New Orleans has provided the backdrop for many successful entrepreneurs but, we need to continue to create the environment that helps them succeed. That means strong government, quality schools and the right blend of support from organizations like The Idea Village. For me, a commitment to the city has always served as my foundation. The passion to succeed through hard work, surrounding myself with quality people and always working to deliver a first-class product are other important ingredients in the recipe for success.

On the pages that follow, you will see a diverse group of New Orleans entrepreneurs. I hope you enjoy discovering how they did it, too.

EMERIL LAGASSE
2009

INTRODUCTION

When I was a girl growing up in New Orleans, one Saturday I needed to shop for a dress for my First Holy Communion. My mother put me in the car and off we went to buy fabric at Krauss. We passed through the hustle and bustle of Canal Street, with its clanging streetcars, decorated store windows and well-dressed shoppers from all parts of the city. Inside Krauss, fancy women's hats were everywhere, displayed next to purses and jewelry that seemed fit for a queen. Riding the escalator was always my favorite thing to do, since this was the first department store in New Orleans with mechanical stairs, as they called them then, not to mention indoor air conditioning. On the second floor were women's clothes and fabrics, but my eyes always strayed to the escalator going up and the black pipes along the ceiling shuffling orders from one floor to the next.

As we left the store and crossed Canal Street, I began to skip. Next on our agenda was lunch. We walked to K&B, the store known by its purple logo, for a hamburger and Coke at the soda fountain. The diner entry was in the front of the store and the aisles of drugstore items in the back. Swiveling stools lined the counter where customers were served sandwiches, sodas and ice cream.

I knew the familiar story would soon come out of my mother's mouth. "Aunt Lettie and I used to come here every week," she said, referring to her older sister. "For only a quarter, we would buy a potato salad sandwich and a Coke."

Then came the funny part.

"Our favorite thing was watching the buck-toothed soda jerk as he called out our order. 'Give the lady a flat fifth', he'd say." Mom always loved to say it just like he did.

"What's a flat fifth?" I would ask.

"It was ice cream served in a flat purple box," she said.

These days, of course, the teeming crowds of shoppers on Canal Street have long disappeared, but now I take my daughter to the new Canal Street, a six-mile corridor of bustling boutiques, coffee shops, bookstores and galleries along Magazine Street. And although my mother's buck-toothed soda jerks are in short supply there, we have established our own shopping traditions in a town known for its colorful local businesses.

"How about Sucré for some sweets?" my daughter might ask after we've browsed the new designs at Mignon Faget and Suzanne Perron.

"Only if we can go to PJ's first," I reply. I usually stop by for a Granita, the high-octane iced drink at the coffee chain that Phyllis Jordan founded here, and have to convince my daughter to traipse about a bit longer in her Feelgoodz flip flops.

As during my childhood rituals along Canal Street, each stop on Magazine Street is a unique shopping or business experience. Innovative talent seems naturally attracted to a city like New Orleans, where art, architecture, food and music provide layers of singular complexities that inspire the character of entrepreneurship. Risk takers, creative thinkers, innovators and visionaries exist hand-in-hand with the more stable and secure corporate types that fill downtown skyscrapers. One can smell adventure in the air on Magazine Street, a whiff of the pioneering business spirit that perhaps has always been attracted to this city.

From its earliest days, New Orleans was a treasure trove of natural resources. Its location at the mouth of the Mississippi River gave rise to commerce and made it a much sought after territory. Several countries fought for control of New Orleans, one of few cities in the United States to have flown under seven flags. Thomas Jefferson, the state's original entrepreneur, realized the importance of the territory and in 1803 entered into one of the largest and riskiest land deals in history, the Louisiana Purchase.

That purchase and the subsequent development turned the city into one of the leading ports of the world. Wharves along the river developed rapidly as trade and commerce thrived. The U. S. Customs House at the foot of Canal Street became one of the most important financial centers in the country. Coffee and bananas filled the docks, brought upriver by the forerunners of food importers such as William B. Reily and Sam Zemurray. Natural wealth turned into physical wealth. Banks and lending institutions opened, mansions were constructed in the Marigny and Garden District, and investment flowed into cotton mills, sugar plantations and the coffee trade.

The New Orleans Cotton Exchange was flourishing and plantations throughout the state were in full production. Although New Orleans

was diverse and had one of the largest communities of free people of color in the South, brutal slavery was the labor that supported this affluent economy. Some owners, however, allowed slaves on their days off to sell hot calas in the street so that they could save up to buy their own freedom. New Orleans' first black neighborhood, the Faubourg Tremé, became a vibrant community with its own newspaper, *The Tribune*. Unfortunately, it wouldn't be long before this progress was reversed, and the clock stood still until the Civil Rights era.

At the same time, small businesses grew exponentially, much as in other cities throughout the country. Retail corridors were built, each centered around a distinct ethnicity, making New Orleans a gumbo pot of languages, skin tones and origins. Creole merchants opened stores and restaurants while living above their shops in the French Quarter. Nearby Canal Street was known as America's widest main street, the Fifth Avenue of the South, where Jewish merchants such as Coleman Adler and Morris Rubenstein opened up jewelry and clothing shops. Along Dryades Street, black New Orleanians shopped at stores such as Handleman's, H&L Green and Porter's Tailoring. German bakers such as George Leidenheimer served hot bread, and Italian grocery stores like Matassa's stood at the corner in every neighborhood. A significant Sicilian population took over the French Market and ran the flower and produce stalls there for decades.

With this prosperity came healthcare development. From early innovators like George Tichenor, who developed an antiseptic still used today, to my own great-grandfather, whose Gelpi forceps continue to help deliver babies, the thriving commerce in New Orleans called for better medical care. Doctors made house calls and received patients in their offices long before Alton Ochsner opened his famous clinic, which paved the way for modern hospitals. Drugstore chains like Sydney Besthoff's K&B spread across the city, perhaps paving the way for the booming biotech industry of such future entrepreneurs as Victor Castellón.

Soon the Great Depression and World War II brought difficult times during the 30's and 40's, but American ingenuity was emboldened in New Orleans, where the hardship inspired innovation. Andrew Higgins designed a boat that many believe won the war for the Allies, while Jerry Goldman discovered a way to secure more cargo on a ship. Pierre Bagur invested in horse-drawn carriages to show visitors the magic of the historic city, while a young artist named Blaine Kern began sculpting plaster of Paris heads for the sides of floats.

Drilling for oil in the Gulf of Mexico initiated a crucial period of growth. Shell, Chevron and Texaco were aided by pioneers such as Alden "Doc" Laborde, designer of one of the first submersible oil rigs. Innovators such as Robert Suggs, who founded Petroleum Helicopters to service the rigs, and Prentiss "P.C." Havens, who offered an easier way to purchase seismic data, flourished in these times. Downtown skyscrapers were filled with new oil and gas companies, both on the exploration and production side as well as on the supply side. Larger-than-life oilmen such as Pat Taylor and Jim Bob Moffett stepped to the forefront of the industry while giving generously to the community in which they lived.

During the late 1960's, city and business leaders met to establish a plan to more formally market the city to tourists. Finally by 1984, the World's Fair established New Orleans as an international brand, conventions started pouring into town, and towering hotels such as the New Orleans Hilton and Marriott were built. The Warehouse District, the staging area for the World's Fair, was renovated into a residential and entertainment zone, where today you can find Emeril's Restaurant and Jonathan Ferrara's art gallery.

At the height of the World's Fair fever, the oil patch dried up, many companies migrated to Texas and economic development began to stagnate in the city. Tourism was the only growth industry, and fewer and fewer local entrepreneurs launched projects. New Orleans business landmarks, including department stores such as D.H. Holmes, Krauss and Maison Blanche, along with food retailers like McKenzies, famous for its doughnuts, and Schwegmann's, where we "made groceries," closed. New Orleanians became accustomed to the nostalgic refrain of Benny Grunch's satirical song: "Ain't 'dere no more."

Today we still rely on our mainstay industries, the port, oil and gas, tourism and healthcare. But for the first time in a long while, there is an upward trend of new entrepreneurs launching businesses in New Orleans.

What exactly is an entrepreneur? Certain words come to mind: *innovator, engineer, designer, original thinker, risk taker, change agent* or *barrier breaker*. Where does an entrepreneur have to begin in order to fit the definition? Does he or she have to start from scratch? To many, the answer is yes. Do entrepreneurs have to instigate change in their field? Again, the answer is often yes.

In choosing the entrepreneurs for this book, a panel of business leaders from The Idea Village studied the classic attributes of entrepreneurs and determined a list of potential participants. Most of the names chosen appear in these pages, although for various reasons, I regret that a few do not. Others were added as I conducted interviews or did research, discovering in the process other significant entrepreneurs or industries that had been overlooked. Many others should be featured in these pages, but there were space limitations. Readers who notice conspicuous gaps should know that other names may be reserved for a future book.

Throughout the pages of *How They Did It: Profiles of New Orleans Entrepreneurs* are stories from the early days of the ventures that illustrate the unrivaled spirit of innovation: stories of traditional and dot.com businesspeople, restaurant magnates, industry leaders and serial entrepreneurs. A few might catch your eye for the changes they created in our city, while others might inspire you by their ability to persevere in the face of adversity. All of these entrepreneurs share a few common qualities: hard work, determination, grit and a passion for what they do. Most are filled with both humility and confidence. Each profile features a unique story, yet taken together, they form an overview of what has made our city such a success.

We begin with the legends: those whose lives created enormous progress in the development of New Orleans. The legends in this book have all passed away, but the gifts they gave us live on. What exactly becomes a legend? Some of them were larger-than-life, while others led modest lives. Each inspired an industry, created change and jobs for our community and affected New Orleanians for generations to come.

The contemporary leaders, most of whom remain at the helm, are those still living successful lives as entrepreneurs. These business people built companies that changed their industries. Many took their companies public. Well-known for their work, they are held in high esteem within their fields and across the business spectrum.

Finally, among the entrepreneurs now on the horizon, we introduce some faces that may be significant to the future growth of the city. The chance that an entrepreneurial start up will make it past ten years is one-in-ten. And the chances that these entrepreneurs will become legends like those at the front of the book may be one-in-a-million. Yet they have taken the risk and stand resolved with a sense of purpose to succeed.

I hope these entrepreneurs inspire you to feel more optimistic about our city's future. For years, the problems we face have drained us of talent and threatened our community. Our public schools were among the worst in the nation, murder was rampant in our streets and corruption, along with a lackadaisical work ethic, were often dismissed as merely part of the city's raffish charm. Other cities thrived while we steadily lost ground.

But citizens have rallied where government has failed. As we watch climbing test scores in reinvigorated public schools, we also prepare for new jobs with the construction of a major healthcare corridor that will be the largest economic development project in the state's history. Entrepreneurial clusters are gaining steam in buildings like The IP, Entrepreneurs Row, Entergy Innovation Center and The Icehouse, while the women affectionately called the Belles of Bayou Road transform the historic African American corridor into a vibrant retail center and John Elstrott lands Tulane's Freeman School of Business as a top five graduate school in the nation for entrepreneurship. The Idea Village, together with other nonprofits whose missions support entrepreneurs, continue to celebrate the appearance of new faces launching bright ideas with a determined spirit.

I would like to thank each of the entrepreneurs represented in this book: the bright ones, the determined and crazy ones, the people who approach a problem differently, the round pegs in the square holes whose can-do spirit is second to none. Their innovation fuels the engine of social and economic changes, and we're lucky to be along for the ride.

I. What Becomes A Legend

Edmund McIlhenny was in the banking business in New Orleans in the mid 1800's. After the war, the food lover and avid gardener left banking to try his hand at adding some spice to the bland diet of the Reconstruction South. Since then, TABASCO™ has been setting the food world on fire. Paul McIlhenny, current president of the company and great-grandson of the founder, talks about the creator of "That Famous Sauce Mr. McIlhenny Makes."

How did your great-grandfather grow up? After his father died, he had to provide for his siblings and went to work for a bank in Baltimore.

What did he know about banking? Nothing. It was on-the-job training.

What brought him to New Orleans? Baltimore experienced a recession and, at the time, New Orleans was a land of opportunity. In 1842, he went to work as a bookkeeper for the Bank of Louisiana, a Creole bank in New Orleans.

How did he do? He worked his way up through the ranks, and by 1857 he was able to purchase five branches of the bank. He became very successful and married Mary Eliza Avery.

What happened? The Civil War broke out and they were forced to retreat to his wife's home on what is now called Avery Island. He tried to return to the banking business but there was no money and carpetbaggers were running the city, so he was unable to return to work in the banking industry.

How did he transition away from banking? In their spare time, he and his wife gardened. She had a rose garden and he tended a vegetable garden that included a variety of very hot peppers. He started making a pepper sauce for his family and their friends. They said, "Why don't you sell this stuff?" So he did, making 358 bottles his first year and distributing them to wholesalers across the country.

What made it different? The process. It's a special variety of pepper that's mashed and ferments for up to three years in white oak barrels, much like fine wine.

Where was it most popular? At first, it was mainly used on raw oysters in oyster houses.

What accelerated the company's early growth? Someone introduced my great-grandfather to a New York grocery wholesaler who helped him spread the business into Europe in the 1870's.

Where did the name TABASCO™ come from? It's a Mexican Indian word that means, "land where the soil is hot and humid" or "place of coral or oyster shell." Grandpere liked the sound of it.

Has the product changed through the years? The formula is basically the same.

What has been the key to your success? We have always been about family. After Edmund's death, his wife oversaw operations along with her eldest son, John Avery McIlhenny. We've had a family member as CEO since day one.

How do you think your great-grandfather viewed success? Well, he never really considered TABASCO™ to be a howling success. Of all of his years in the Tabasco business, he continued to think of his banking career as more successful.

How many bottles can you now make in a day? 700,000.

DON'T RUSH A GOOD THING

George Leidenheimer emigrated to New Orleans from Deidesheim, Germany, where his family had a long baking tradition. In 1896, he opened Leidenheimer Bakery, a family business that is now in its fourth generation. His grandson Robert J. Whann III shares Leidenheimer's secret to serving delicious French bread.

Describe George Leidenheimer. He was a stocky, barrel-chested man who could easily heft a 100-pound sack of flour over his shoulder.

Where did he live? When the bakery started, he and my grandmother lived above the bakery.

How was competition in 1896? There were over 200 bakeries listed in the phone books at that time. The original plant was on Dryades at Melpomene Street. Leidenheimer had an agreement with Sunrise Bakery that Canal Street would be the delivery dividing line. Sunrise would serve the French Quarter and below, and Leidenheimer would serve the other side of Canal and above. Certainly such an agreement would be illegal today.

Is baking an art form? Baking is a mixture of science and art. Time and temperature are critical, but skilled hands are also very important.

When did the new plant open? In 1905, and it was innovative because it featured windows, which were unheard of in bakeries at that time. Therefore, it was billed "The Daylight Bakery."

What innovations were made to modernize? We used rack ovens, which generated their own steam. We also installed a tunnel oven that used a hearth-baking process similar to that used by my grandfather. Early on, we experimented with using a retarder.

What does a retarder do? A retarder is a cooler that stops dough from rising and allows it to be baked at a later time.

How did your name become synonymous with French bread? Leidenheimer tapered back on production of the heavy German breads to which he was accustomed in order to produce a product that would complement New Orleans' unique cuisine. Thankfully, he made the right choice.

What fascinating ways has the bread been eaten throughout the years? In my mother's day, they used to hollow out the heel, or end, of the bread and pour condensed milk in it.

Have you seen some odd blends on sandwiches? I once saw a red bean and blackened pork chop po-boy, which seems strange to me, though it's probably pretty good. And I don't think any other city in America makes sandwiches using potatoes and roast beef drippings, which was purportedly the original po-boy.

What famous teeth have bitten into your bread? Presidents, popes and other world leaders, business tycoons, Carnival kings and queens and anyone fortunate enough to dine in our wonderful New Orleans restaurants, which I think are the finest in the world.

Baking secrets? In order to get that crispness to the bread once it has been frozen, DO NOT THAW IT! That will take all the moisture out of the bread. Place the frozen bread directly in a preheated oven at 350 degrees. To reheat fresh bread that has been stored in a plastic bag, run your hand under water and rub it over the bread. Put the bread back into a preheated oven at 350 degrees until the crust is crispy.

What is your family's favorite way to eat your bread? Hot out of the oven with butter, butter, butter and more butter.

EVERYTHING AND EVERYONE DEPENDS ON THE SOIL

Photo Courtesy of the Zemuarry Family

Sam Zemurray began working as a young boy selling ripe bananas coming into the docks of Mobile, Alabama. Pursuing his passion, he later started the Cuyamel Fruit Company. In 1929, Cuyamel merged with United Fruit Company, another banana importer, and Zemurray emerged as president. United Fruit eventually controlled nearly a half-mile of dock space at the Port of New Orleans. Grandson, Sam Zemurray III, and great-granddaughter, Stephanie Feoli, share their knowledge of "Sam the Banana Man."

How did Sam get his nickname? As a young man, he decided to put the "ripes" (ripe bananas that were discarded) on a train from Mobile to Selma, Alabama, where he lived with his uncle. He wired telegraph operators along the way to let the local grocers know that he was coming and promised them a free bunch if they would buy his bananas. Soon they were all waiting for his arrival and would say, "Sam the Banana Man is coming."

What got him interested in owning his own business? He traveled to Puerto Cortes, Honduras, and eventually bought land on the Cuyamel River. The banana business meant more than just a profession to him. He felt a deep connection to the land.

What distinguished his product? Believing everything and everyone depended on the soil.

How did he accelerate growth? With several new ideas: a system of large-scale irrigation, selective pruning and by propping the banana trees up with bamboo poles to protect the fruit.

What did he consider his best innovation? His method of increasing production by stilting. Instead of protecting the farms not under cultivation from floodwaters, he let the floods overflow. Years later, when the land had drained, the banana trees were planted and their production doubled from the previous year.

Did he continue to be a risk taker? Yes, in 1935 when the plantations were threatened by Sigatoka (a disease that shrinks the banana fruit), he risked millions and saved the business by experimenting with a new yet unproven treatment developed by a scientist.

How did he reward employees' achievement? After the Depression, the company recovered from its losses under his direction. Once profitable, his employees were paid wages three to five times higher than other companies and given free housing. The only thing he expected from them was results.

What was your grandfather like as a person? Sam had an engaging, impressive personality, was strong-spirited and physically imposing. He would practice fasting, sometimes up to two weeks, only taking liquids and would meditate before coming back to work, always ready and with more energy.

He became a huge philanthropist? Yes, but he liked to be anonymous in his giving.

What were his most marked characteristics? Tenacity, self-discipline, humility and, mostly, he was a great judge of character and wise in human nature.

What was he most passionate about? His work and education. He funded a chair at Harvard and an agricultural school in Honduras.

Did he have an affinity for Latin America? He spoke three languages: Russian, Spanish and English, but Spanish was his favorite. He had businesses in nine countries and traveled frequently by *lomo de mula* through Central America. It was important for him to feel close to the people.

Did he have a motto? What is best for the country we operate in is best for the company.

QUICK SALES, SMALL PROFITS
AND CASH TRANSACTIONS

Photo Courtesy of Boatner Reily

William B. Reily spent part of his childhood clerking at a county grocery store in Bastrop, Louisiana. By 1887, he had saved enough money to open his own grocery. Sensing an increased demand for coffee, he eventually moved to New Orleans to roast, grind, package and distribute canned coffee. Years later, the Luzianne brand was the first to blend a tea for the purpose of serving it with ice. Boatner Reily, grandson of William B. Reily, reflects on the birth of the Luzianne brand and Reily Foods, which today produces and distributes over 100 brands.

How would you describe your grandfather? He was known to be a very courteous and levelheaded man with a can-do spirit.

How did he get his start? Clerking at a grocery store.

Did he meet resistance when he opened his first store? It was assumed that he would fail.

What business qualities did he possess? He was an energetic, hard worker who believed in quick sales, small profits and cash transactions. Many wealthy people who were used to a merchant carrying their credit on the books were unhappy about having to pay cash, but they still gave him the business.

What kind of early growth did he experience? His store was so successful that he moved to Monroe, Louisiana and opened a distinctive grocery wholesale business there.

What happened next? The French explorers had introduced coffee in the 1700's and there was growing demand for it. He decided to move to New Orleans to enter into the business of canned coffee.

What was the competitive landscape? Several coffee roasting plants began to crop up close to Café du Monde, making it a crowded market.

What made his plant different? Reily, Taylor & Company, the original name, opened as a more modern coffee roasting and tea importing plant.

How did they roast coffee in the early 1900's? First, they cleaned and separated whole beans from broken beans.

Then, like beans were put in iron cylinders to roast and achieve equality in the roasting, which was considered a superior method to coffee roasted by a cook. At the time, 85% of all imported coffee beans passed through New Orleans, ensuring first-dibs of the finest beans available.

In the early 1900's there was a stock market panic followed by the yellow fever epidemic. How did your grandfather survive this challenging time? He was fortunate to have a solid business reputation and was able to bring in green coffee importer, Jacob Aron, as an investor.

What became of that pairing? It began a partnership that has now lasted over 100 years.

How did the company help introduce iced tea? Ice was being used more frequently in drinks and we decided to brew a tea solely for that purpose.

What was the initial product called? Luzianne Red Label.

Can you share the secret recipe? Less tannin in the tea, making it better for iced tea.

What are your current brands? We have over 100 Reily Foods Company brands, including CDM coffee, Blue Plate Mayonnaise, Standard Office Coffee Service Co., Swan's Down cake flour, chili kits, salad dressings and fat-free brownie mixes.

What has been the key to your success? Our focus on marketing and consumer loyalty to our brands.

Dr. George Tichenor, known as the pioneer of antiseptic surgery, was wounded in battle and faced the amputation of a limb. Against standard medical advice, he poured a liquid that he had recently concocted onto his leg and was healed. Today Dr. Tichenor's Antiseptic is used worldwide on a variety of ailments. Parker LeCorgne, the current president of the company and great-grandson of its founder, Arthur Parker, talks about the inventor, Dr. Tichenor.

Where did Dr. Tichenor grow up? Kentucky.

Where did he go to school? He started out in public school but ran away from home after his mother died.

What was his first job? One of his first jobs was manufacturing gun powder.

Was he a chemist? Yes, and a surgeon.

How did he come up with this antiseptic? He was experimenting with alcohol in an attempt to sterilize and help heal wounds.

Was he ever injured? Twice in the war. One of those times his doctor recommended he have his leg amputated, and he didn't want to do that. Friends snuck him out of the hospital at night, so he could avoid the amputation.

What year did he open the business? Dr. Tichenor patented the formula in 1883 as Dr. Tichenor's Patent Medicine. It wasn't until 1905 that the product was manufactured and sold by the Dr. G.H. Tichenor Antiseptic Company in New Orleans after contracting with my great-grandfather, Arthur Parker.

What are some of the ingredients besides alcohol? Oil of peppermint and Arnica.

How was it used? For internal and external ailments.

Such as? Cuts, scrapes, sore throats, insect bites, bad breath, stomach problems, sore muscles, shaving, wound care, burns, bruises, colic, cramps and cholera.

Any other common uses? A lot of people like to rub it on their feet to ward off germs. The peppermint oil also delivers a cool, "freshening" sensation.

Did Dr. Tichenor understand the significance of his invention? He did not realize he was pioneering the field of surgery, but he knew his product was different and worthy.

What was his nature? He was hard-headed and hard working, but was a pioneer in many different areas.

Such as? He discovered permanganate of potash for snakebites, he was the first to successfully treat spinal meningitis and he perfected a method of grafting. Oddly, he also became knowledgeable of our waterways and is credited with the development of the spillway.

Where is the company now? We produce over a million bottles of Dr. Tichenor's a year for devoted customers all over the world.

Has it changed much through the years? No. It is still the same amber-colored, peppermint-flavored, powerful liquid antiseptic.

Your favorite tagline? Dr. Tichenor's - It's like having a medicine cabinet in a bottle.

Anything that it's not good for? There have been reports of rather exotic applications which are not recommended.

What happens to someone who gargles without adding water? They spit faster than ever.

Tichenor's motto? Gargle, Wince, Repeat.

17

PURPLE ON THE OUTSIDE

Sydney Besthoff approached Gustave Katz about opening a pharmacy in downtown New Orleans. In 1895, they opened the doors to the first Katz & Besthoff, affectionately known as K&B. Throughout the 20th century, the business grew to nearly 200 stores and 5,000 employees before it was sold in 1997. Sydney Besthoff III shares how his grandfather developed the brand fondly called the "purple dragon."

Describe your grandfather's childhood. He was raised in Memphis in a Jewish Orphanage Asylum along with his sister.

What brought him to New Orleans? He came to marry my grandmother, Florence Stich.

What were his plans? He graduated from pharmacy school and early on envisioned a chain of drug stores.

How did he begin? He met Gus Katz, a pharmacist like my grandfather, who already had a store. Katz was operating uptown and wanted to open a store downtown, so they formed a partnership.

Where was the first store? On Canal Street, a celebrated shopping corridor at the time.

Did they have a tagline? "Only the Best."

How were early sales? Patrons followed Gus Katz, and young people hung out at the soda fountain. Many of their families followed.

How was this pharmacy different? They wanted to be known for quality and good sanitation. They made soda girls wear hairnets, soda men wear caps and they inspected the soda fountain daily.

What type of innovation did they bring to pharmacies? They created a double-check system in which one pharmacist would fill the order, and the other would check it for accuracy. He also formed a credit system at stores on Canal Street known as the New Orleans Shopper Card. This later turned into a K&B credit card.

What was your grandfather's nature? He was a people person who loved shaking hands and meeting new people.

What about his business acumen? He was very knowledgeable about business and had a strong belief that expansion could work.

How did the K&B purple come about? A local retailer ordered purple paper and found the color too intense. The salesman offered it to my grandfather for a cheap price, so he took it.

It changed your tagline? Yes. We added, "If it's purple on the outside, it's only the best from Katz & Besthoff."

What were some of your unique products? Wine called Yendis (a variation of Sydney backwards), K&B ice cream, hair rollers, Coca-Cola – a hot item at the time - and the list goes on.

What helped accelerate your growth? The manufacturing and selling of our ice creams. We went from selling flat fifths, slim boxes that fit in the smaller freezer compartments of old-style refrigerators, to selling and delivering larger quantities in more modern packaging.

Where are the K&B signature products now? Most were sold for charity.

What are you nostalgic for? The K&B connection that existed between employees and the long list of loyal customers.

WHEN TO PUT THE PRESSURE ON AND WHEN TO TAKE IT OFF

Arthur and Henry Boh created a construction company at the turn of the century to handle the demands of a major city in development. Over a century later, Boh Brothers Construction serves as one of the largest contractors in the South. Reflecting on the company that has built major bridges, highways and flood protection systems, Henry's grandson, Robert Boh, looks back.

What did New Orleans look like when the company began? The city was the largest in the South, so a lot of people were moving in and a lot of construction was taking place.

Who started the company? Arthur was the lead, and Henry joined right after.

What was Arthur's background? He was a draftsman, one of seven at the Sewerage and Water Board.

What opportunity did Arthur see? Even though it was a big city, New Orleans was still behind the times in terms of development. Arthur saw this as a chance to move into construction.

When was he awarded his first job? In 1909. It was for four residential buildings on what is now South Jefferson Davis Parkway.

Was the bulk of construction residential then? It was primarily residential. It wasn't until World War I that the company saw an opening and moved into something few companies were focused on: underground utilities and streets.

What was the first major project? Creating the city's first thoroughfare, the eight-lane Airline Highway (now Airline Drive).

What was their competitive advantage? We become a diversified civil contractor.

What was considered a long pile drive? 200 feet for One Shell Square. It was historic at the time.

Did they ever discover anything underground? While driving piles for the Superdome, we found a cemetery underneath that was built during the yellow fever epidemic.

So there are ghosts under the Superdome? No comment.

How did they handle challenges? As my grandfather always said, "You have to know when to put the pressure on and when to take it off."

How many bridges have you built in New Orleans? We built 29 of the 31 overpasses in the city.

Did you build any of the city's subdivisions? In the 1950's we built Gentilly Woods, and later we built Eastover and English Turn.

How does Boh Bros continuously satisfy customers? Our core purpose is to honorably serve our communities.

Is it still only buildings, highways and bridges? We now do industrial work, power plants and other types of major projects.

How many employees do you have? Currently 1,500, many of whom are multi-generational family members, and all of whom we value, honor and respect. We turned 100 years old in 2009.

Henry's passion? He believed everything should be about the field. If someone bought office furniture, he asked if the piece could dig a hole.

Did they have a motto? When you give your word, you've got to stand behind it.

TAKE RISKS IN BUSINESS

William Burkenroad was an impoverished young boy when he came to New Orleans from Goodman, Mississippi. In the pursuit of opportunity, he eventually partnered with Jacob Aron in the coffee and commodity business, and founded the Green Coffee Association of New Orleans in 1923. Two of his great-grandsons, Steve Usdin and Bobby Bories, explain more about the man that started an empire.

What was life like for your great-grandfather growing up? At the age of 14, he dropped out of school to support his family, including six siblings. He never graduated from high school or college.

Did that hinder him? No. He was self-educated, even following the theories of Einstein and the laws of relativity, as well as many business philosophies that were popular in his time.

What was his first business venture? A wholesale grocery company known as Burkenroad and Goldsmith.

How did he get involved in the coffee business? Through his mentor, Jacob Aron, who had decided that to develop quickly into a sizable coffee and commodity business, they should open a New York office. Aron asked our great-grandfather to join his firm, J. Aron & Company, as a partner and run its New Orleans office. In 1911, Aron moved to New York, and Burkenroad assumed responsibility in New Orleans.

When did the company go into business with William B. Reily? The story goes that during an economic downturn William B. Reily came to their office and asked a man sweeping the room if he could see William Burkenroad. He was told by the man sweeping to come back in an hour. When he came back, he discovered it was the same man.

How long did that partnership last? They were partners for a long time, even when Reily suffered a major fire. Our great-grandfather and Jacob Aron honored their deal with Reily and stayed true to their word.

After Jacob Aron mentored him, did Burkenroad mentor others? Yes. He worked to assist many in the business community, including some in his own family.

Such as? He was a source of great wisdom to his son-in-law, Leo Weil, who at 18 years old began to tinker with air conditioning and heating. Weil was an electrical engineer by training, who pioneered the installation of central air conditioning throughout the country.

How did Leo Weil innovate? He air-conditioned the first department store in the country, Krauss Department Store on Canal Street. In fact, he was one of the first in the country to develop central air conditioning for large buildings.

What was Burkenroad's greatest business asset? He had a strong reputation as a consensus builder.

To what do you credit his success? He combined good judgement with a willingness to take risks in business, including his purchase of a sugar refinery in Supreme, Louisiana. Eventually, it became one of the largest in the state, along with the American, Godchaux and Colonial refineries.

What lessons did your great-grandfather teach you? The importance of integrity, good judgment, generosity and trustworthiness.

FEELING FOR THE TRENDS

Sam Pulitzer was one of 12 children when he was sent to live in a Jewish orphanage. Learning how to sell products at an early age, he often dreamed of owning his own business. After working for a tie company, he opened Wembley Ties, which would eventually become an industry leader and sell ties to over 12,000 retailers. His son, Sidney Pulitzer, now an adjunct professor teaching entrepreneurship at Tulane, remembers his father.

What was your father's childhood like? He was one of 12 children. After his parents died, he and his brothers were sent to live in an orphanage.

What was his first job? When my father graduated from the eighth grade, there were no child labor laws, so he went to work for the railroad.

What do you remember about him? He was courageous and driven by ambition to do better.

When did he open his own business? He and his brother got a truck, went down to the swamp to buy muskrat furs, and sold them in New Orleans, but the flood of 1927 wiped the muskrats out.

What did he do then? He gathered old batteries from gas stations, chopped them open, then melted down the lead and sold it.

How did he get interested in ties? One of his brothers sold ties in New York and sent some down for my father to sell. Everyone wore ties then.

What was his greatest innovation? His brother bought a suit made of Australian mohair and English wool, spun together in a fabric that didn't wrinkle. At that time, ties wrinkled, so my dad cut the back out of that coat and made the first wrinkle-proof necktie.

What year did he open? 1924. I asked him what the Depression was like and he said they were so poor he didn't notice the difference.

What was his strength in business? Dad understood finance.

How did he define success? As an orphan, he defined it by having enough money to have food on his table, clothes to wear and a new car.

What was his business philosophy? It was actually my mother who suggested he sell to everyone at a single, fair price. "One price to everybody" became his mantra.

What accelerated the company's growth? Three things: experience, courage and the ability to understand people, money, our product and the customer.

What was your father's nature? He was generous but a tough businessman who didn't hesitate to dress someone down.

What did he teach you? Finance, discipline and he urged me to be humble and hungry. I have trouble with the humble part.

Keys to the company's success? You have to have a feeling for the trends and analyze what sells and what doesn't.

How did your father train you? He trained me for three years and then let me design embroidered neckware. In the embroidery department, I brought a 300% increase in sales. By my fourth year, I did all of the buying and eventually ran the business.

How big did you get? We reached $86 million in sales.

How many ties is that? Enough to go around the earth nine times.

Lessons learned from your father? He loved the business. He worked until the week before he died.

NOTHING MORE CERTAIN IN LIFE
THAN CHANGE

Joseph Jones enjoyed a successful law practice but was fascinated by business. Amidst the Depression in 1933, the entrepreneurial lawyer co-founded Canal Barge Company with a single barge. Today, the company is one of the largest and most diverse privately-owned marine transportation companies in the United States. Current president Merritt Lane, who owns the company with his siblings and cousins, remembers his grandfather.

Describe your grandfather's childhood. He grew up in New Orleans as an only child in a family with a tradition of service and leadership. His great-grandfather was the first Episcopal Bishop of Louisiana and a founder of the University of the South. His father and grandfather were both well-known physicians who made major contributions to the eradication of Yellow Fever in the city. His mother was active and worked towards progressing women's rights. This service and civic-mindedness greatly influenced Joe.

What was his nature? He was positive, generous and befriended those of high character. A sports enthusiast who played "scrub" tackle for Tulane, he supported their athletics and the city's attempts to land a professional football team.

Did he enlist in the war? No, he was too old, but he moved to D.C. to work for the State Department.

And after the war? He returned to Jones Walker, the law firm he formed in 1937, which grew rapidly and remains one of the largest in the Gulf South.

Why did he invest in the maritime industry? He saw the barge business as a great inflation hedge and, essentially as "floating real estate." He was convinced that marine transportation would become more important to the United States as the economy grew.

How did he begin? With a single barge, the CBC-1. Relying on partners and key staff for their operational know-how, they incorporated in 1933.

During the Depression? Yes, the day after the repeal of Prohibition. Unemployment was about 25%.

What is the significance of 'Canal Barge'? We originally operated a single barge in the canal that is now the Gulf Intracoastal Waterway.

Why inland waterways? It was clear to him that as our economy grew, there would be a need for more power generation, an expansion of the refining and chemical industries and an increase in international trade. They would need American-built, owned and manned ships for movement between United States ports.

What inspired him? Building strong institutions with good people and providing great service. He would be proud that we are one of the nation's leading marine transportation companies.

His greatest assets? He was a hard worker, had tremendous drive and was forthright facing challenges.

Any public policy work? As head of the National Waterways Conference, he lobbied Congress not to impose fees on companies that shipped products by barge and who relied on government investment in locks and dams to make the waterways navigable.

Was he engaged locally? He was President of Tulane's Board from 1950, leading it through integration and improving its national ranking, until he died tragically with his wife in a fire in 1963. A past-President of the Bureau of Governmental Research and the New Orleans Bar Association, he was active in many civic organizations.

His business philosophy? Believe in good people, successful relationships, always do the right thing and build equity through continuous reinvestment.

And his motto? There is nothing more certain in life than change.

BRINGING HOME A PIECE OF NEW ORLEANS

Pierre Bagur was a young man with a wife and four children trying to make it through the Depression when he developed his own recipe for pralines. With the money from the sales of pralines, he then created a horse-drawn carriage business in the French Quarter. Aimée Bagur, his granddaughter, shares the stories that her Aunts Diane and Yvette and Uncle Jacques have told her of their father's nurturing love of the city through the development of tourism.

Describe Pierre. Tiny with a theatrical flair.

How did your grandfather begin? Out of necessity during the Depression. He was the instigator, but the whole immediate family participated. He started selling the pralines at a magazine stand called Little Pierre's operated by his two sons, Pierre Jr. and Jacques, at Royal and St. Louis streets, where the Royal Orleans Hotel is today. The cash register was a shoe box, and selling postcards inspired the idea of packaging pralines as souvenirs. The mail order business started at this stand.

Did he only sell there? The pralines were also sold in the Creole section of Esplanade Avenue. On all Saints Day and All Souls Day, the pralines would be sold in the cemeteries.

When did he open a shop? It was a tiny stall in the open air produce section of the French Market. Customers could select pralines, dolls and cotton bales colorfully displayed in every conceivable space of the stall. He built a hinged door that could be pulled down at closing time. In that same year, he and his sons turned Little Pierre's into a log cabin type structure, where they also sold pralines.

What was the first store called? Ye Old Candy Shoppe. The name was changed to Aunt Sally's at the end of the 30's.

His secret praline recipe? They were crispy and delicate, with Louisiana pecans and choice ribbon-cane sugar from the cane fields.

How did he succeed? He saw that visitors might want to bring home a piece of New Orleans. Packaged pralines were an inexpensive item easily mailed or taken home in a suitcase.

How did he catch his customers' eyes? Art. The family was artistic. They created all of the packaging, jam crates, cotton bales and artifacts. My grandmother sewed handmade dolls of historical figures to sell in the shops.

The dolls and figures were famous. My grandmother and aunts would spend hours in the Cabildo making drawings for the little statues and the dolls. The statues were of plaster of Paris and the dolls were made of fabric, featuring hand-painted faces and fine needlework costuming.

Your grandfather is also credited with starting the horse-drawn carriage trade. When my grandparents went to St. Augustine, Florida, they were charmed by the buggies there. Pierre began a collection that was eventually incorporated into the business. He and his sons reconstructed, repainted and reupholstered old surreys and carriages that they used in parades and for tours. Tours were given in the French Quarter and out to Lake Pontchartrain.

Aunt Sally's grew? A number of locations appeared in the 40's and 50's. The most famous was the log cabin on Royal, plus the one next to Café du Monde still open today.

What was the key to his success? Our cooks, Iola Thomas, her mother, and her daughter, Edna Mae Francis, made pralines of perfection. Mail order was important, as were kitchens inside the stores, where visitors could watch pralines being made.

IF YOU HAVE AN IDEA, COME TO ME

Andrew J. Higgins, inventor of the Higgins Landing Craft used on the beaches at Normandy, is credited with winning World War II for the United States by General Dwight D. Eisenhower. Higgins built Higgins Industries in 1938, producing over 20,000 boats during the war and holding over 30 patents related to amphibious boats and vehicles. Biographer Jerry Strahan discusses Higgins' early years.

As a child he delivered papers and cut grass? Yes, and turned those into enterprises.

Did he have a nickname? Yes. The press occasionally called him "The-Hell-It-Can't Higgins."

What made him so successful? His ability to deal with people. He could relate to the average guy like he could relate to FDR.

Did he promote ingenuity? His door was always open. He would tell his workers, "If you have an idea, come to me."

What was the result? Ideas flowed. It really displayed his managerial genius.

Describe his business style. He was quick to admit his shortcomings and never fearful of hiring someone more intelligent than he was.

He first had a lumber company? Yes. He collected lumber being tossed away in France, milled it and sold it as pecky cypress during the Florida building boom.

How did he move from lumber to the boat business? Raw logs weren't selling. He had the logs cut and one of his engineers designed a boat using the logs.

Did he have a source of inspiration? He had what he called an "Imagineer" in a man named John Poche. Poche had no form of schooling, but was an artist. Higgins would describe his idea, Poche would draw a picture and then Higgins would walk it over to his engineers and say, "Build it." That's how many of his ideas were born.

How did he structure his boat business? He always built fixed-fee, never cost plus. He believed his job was not to make a profit, but to win the war.

Did he think his boats were vital? The Navy didn't believe they needed them, but he believed in them and built them anyway.

Where did he build the boats? He built a plant on City Park Avenue, but soon outgrew it. Without permission, he expanded onto Hope Cemetery. He said, "After the war, then we will figure this out."

How did he train sailors to use the boats? He set up a boat school and trained 30,000 men.

Did he have a special way of sending them off? Before they shipped out, he would throw parties at the Blue Room. When the parties became too large, he moved them to West End. He did this out of his own pocket.

What were his greatest assets? He was a production and design genius. In normal times, he might have been an average businessman. Wars made him. Hurricanes destroyed him.

What do you think he would consider his greatest achievement? Building the boats that allowed for the Normandy invasion, which in turn saved lives and brought victory to the United States. Second to that was building the airborne droppable light boat designed to save lives.

His personal philosophy? Don't wait for opportunity to knock, kick the door down.

USE MONEY TO MAKE MONEY

James Viavant and his co-founders, Harry Koch and Perry Ellis, started Avondale Marine Ways, Inc. in 1938 with an old pair of railway rails and an idea for a ship cleaning and repair business. This soon transitioned into shipbuilding as a way to keep their workers busy in between the more lucrative repair jobs. From there, Avondale became one of the Navy's largest shipbuilding contractors. Viavant's daughter, Barbara Johnsen, reflects on her father's love for building a business.

Did your father go to college? No. His father died when he was 19, and his mother had passed before that, so after graduating from Warren Easton High School he went to work for a bank to support his five brothers and sisters. That's how he learned to use money to make money.

How did he start his business? He was originally in the business of cleaning ships. The Navy decided to relocate the dock that they had been using to get the ships out of the water to Hawaii, so they needed a new way to get the ships out of the water.

So he was at a crossroads? Yes, but an ex-riverboat captain, Harry Koch, told my father about a pair of railway rails that went down into the Mississippi River and had been used to load rail cars onto the barges. They realized if they could rent those rails, they could use them to pull the ships up.

How did he know it would work? Koch was also a diver. He went down and inspected the rails and they looked good.

What did your father do? He approached the oil company that had the lease on the facility and they agreed to let him have the remaining three years on the lease for $75 a month.

What was his expertise? He knew finances so he became the money man.

Who else was involved? Perry Ellis joined my father and Harry in January of 1938. Harry was president, Perry was vice president and daddy was secretary/treasurer. As equal partners, they each put in $5,000 and dubbed the company Avondale Marine Ways.

How did the company grow? They built a second rail to accommodate wider barges and constructed a steel cradle for hauling the ships out of the water using heavy I-beams that were leftover from the construction of the Lake Pontchartrain Bridge.

What changes did this growth bring? They knew they needed someone with more experience in marine repair and construction. They approached Alex Bull about joining them and three became four.

When did the company take off? When they began bidding on Navy contracts during World War II. I remember him flying to Washington to fight for the contracts. Their first major one came in 1941 and called for the manufacturing of four tugboats. They just kept growing from there.

How did he relate to his employees? He liked to make a livelihood for them. He could name each one of them and they were always coming to the house. We were all like family.

What did your father enjoy? He was a very easy-going, down-to-earth man, and a hunter and fisherman who loved the outdoors.

What made him most proud? He really enjoyed growing companies and called it "the greatest game in town." Later, after he sold Avondale, he bought Zatarain's, which was bankrupt at the time, and successfully built that up again.

What qualities helped him suceed? He was a creative spirit.

A LIFELONG CRUSADE

Dr. Alton Ochsner led a lifelong crusade against cigarettes and their harmful effects. Now he is recognized as the first person to discover the link between cigarettes and lung cancer as well as one of the five physicians responsible for creating Ochsner Clinic in 1942, a precursor to the modern-day hospital. His son, Dr. John L. Ochsner, a cardiothoracic heart surgeon and also a medical pioneer, talks about his father's early years.

Where was your father raised? In the Dakota Territory, now South Dakota, in a mud house. There were six daughters, and he was the only boy. His parents opened a store and a school.

Did he work? He stocked the shelves at the store and saved enough money to go to college and later to medical school.

What type of medicine did he specialize in? His work was general surgery. In that day, this meant he did everything.

How did the idea of Ochsner Clinic develop? At the time, physicians had to refer patients across town to one another. A group of five physicians, my father included, came up with the concept of bringing specialists together in one building where they could more easily care for and refer their patients.

How did they begin? They borrowed money, organized a staff of 19 and in 1941, three weeks before the outbreak of World War II, established the Ochsner Clinic Associates and Ochsner Clinic, Inc.

Why two different organizations? They wanted to start a non-profit so that people could donate tax-free. These donations would then pay for the foundation and promote research and teaching.

What accelerated their early growth? The timing was good because health insurance was beginning to cover more people, followed by Medicare and Medicaid in the 1960's and an explosion in medical research. But perhaps more important was the basic fact that these five doctors had exceptional reputations. They served as chairmen of their specialization societies and presidents of medical boards.

His inspiration? He was in love with medicine.

How did he discover the link between cigarettes and lung cancer? As a medical student, a pathologist called his students into an autopsy: cancer of the lung. Alton never did see lung cancer again until he arrived in New Orleans. Here he saw case after case, with the common link being the Picayune cigarettes so popular in the area. He said, "You don't have to be a genius to figure this out."

So he began a war against smoking? Airlines used to give cigarettes away on flights. When National Airlines asked my father to sit on their board, he told them he wouldn't unless they stopped this practice. He persuaded them to make one row non-smoking. Then one row turned into two and so on.

What did people think of his quest? Dr. Everett Graham, his professor, warned him that his colleagues were beginning to think of him as a kook. Years later, Dr. Graham contracted lung cancer himself. He joined in the crusade against smoking and it was in his labs that many experiments to determine the effects of cigarettes were conducted.

What major changes came from Ochsner? It was a hospital of firsts: the first integrated hospital in the South, the first institution in the country to be non-smoking, the first to have a family waiting room and the first to offer post-op care.

The results? We are now seven hospitals, 35 centers, 700 physicians in 80 specialties. We are the largest employer in the state with 11,000 employees.

The key to your father's success? Persistence, hard work and an aversion to anything crooked.

MIXES EASY, JUST ADD HARD WORK

Stephen Goldring moved to New Orleans in 1944 and opened Magnolia Liquor Company. In 1948, he acquired Sazerac Company, a bottler of beverage alcohol, and a few years later began selling Taaka Vodka, the third brand of vodka to be introduced in the United States. Today, his son, Bill Goldring, presides over the Sazerac Company, America's largest distiller, as well as Republic Beverage Company and Crescent Crown Distributing Company, the nation's second-largest wholesaler of liquor, wine and beer.

How did your father begin? When Prohibition ended in Florida in 1939, he founded a wholesale wine and liquor company, became a bottler of wine and owned a small barroom.

What led to his growth? He acquired franchises for brands that had little consumer recognition.

His greatest strength? Finance and operations.

What lessons did you learn from him? Surround yourself with highly intelligent people who are smarter than you, take care of your people as they are your greatest assets, turn over responsibilities and do not micromanage.

Yet he wanted you to work hard? He told me to work hard and never be a loafer.

Did he have a partner? Yes, Malcolm Woldenberg, Seagram's third employee in the United States.

What brands are you known for? Grey Goose, Chivas Regal, Jack Daniels, Absolut, Bombay, Bacardi, Jagermeister and Taaka Vodka.

There's a well-known tagline to Taaka Vodka. Since 1958, the tag has been the same — "mixes easy, just add people."

Did a lot of people drink Vodka in the 1950's? Actually, if you drank vodka during the McCarthy hearings, you were considered a communist.

What was the company's first major acquisition? We purchased the Sazerac Company in 1948. Today it is international and the largest American distiller.

What was the company like when you started? It was 1964, there were 200 employees and my office was a closet.

What was your first job? I sold soft drinks at Tulane Stadium, then graduated to programs and seats.

When did you start running the business? When I was 29 years old.

How did you take the company to the next level? We acquired wholesale companies in other states.

Such as? In 1982, we entered the beer business by acquiring the Coors franchise in opening Crescent Crown. In 1991, we bought our first distillery in Kentucky and now own three additional distilleries there, as well as one in Virginia. Our first major acquisition outside of Louisiana came in 1996 when we moved into Texas.

What are the most important tools to master in your industry? Marketing and distribution.

What's your favorite drink? Espresso.

What excites you? The people, because they come from all walks of life and that makes business fun.

Define success. Health, happiness and friendships.

Your business philosophy? Whatever must be done tomorrow can be finished today.

Advice for emerging entrepreneurs? Focus on growth and remember that only results count.

A TREMENDOUS LOVE OF PEOPLE

Photo Courtesy of the Bollinger Family

Donald Bollinger graduated from high school at the height of the Depression. Using skills he learned from his father, he worked as a machinist at Barker Barge Line. After 11 years, Barker passed away leaving Bollinger $10,000 in recognition of his leadership. With that and his savings, Bollinger opened Bollinger Machine Shop and Shipyard in 1946. He later bought his first World War II warehouse along the banks of Bayou Lafourche. While working in the oil industry, the machine business grew too, with a boat construction and repair business. Donald's son, Boysie Bollinger, who now sits at the head of the company, explains the early years.

Was your father industrious? Very industrious. He worked constantly, but always took time for family.

When did he become interested in boats? His father worked in a shipyard and taught his boys the skills to build and repair commercial vessels. He lived in South Louisiana, which was dominated with water and boats.

Where did he build his first boats? Along the banks of Bayou Lafourche, just south of Lockport.

What skills did your father acquire in the early years? He learned to be a machinist and to weld. He also learned business skills from his boss.

What was his first job? Working for Barker Barge Line, the same place where his dad worked. Mr. Barker took dad under his wing and made him somewhat of an understudy.

Why did he open his own boat business? When the owner died after World War II, his heirs didn't want to grow the business. My father wanted to be involved with a growing company, so he left and opened his own.

His strength in the company's early development? He was good at looking at the opportunities and risks, greatly understood profits and losses and invested his earnings right back into the business.

How did the company evolve? Right after the war, the oil and gas business in Louisiana was taking off. He grew with it and took advantage of the fact that boats were the key to the growing oil and gas business in Louisiana. He began repairing vessels and eventually began building them for this new industry.

Were boats built as the company grew? He had the technical ability to build boats, but he couldn't do it alone. He grew a talented and loyal workforce to build them.

What attribute served him best? His word was his bond. He always wanted to learn, listen to his customers and then give them quality at a reasonable price.

What type of leader was he? He was a good listener, smart at reading people and very inclusive, with a unique ability to pull people together. It never had to be his way, as long as all were pulling in the right direction.

Keys to his success? He would say optimism, intelligence and that God was on his side.

What did he look for in employees? Good, honest, hardworking people to help build the company. He treated them fairly but appreciated them as individuals.

Where is the company now? It's grown into the largest non-naval shipyard in the United States. We operate 13 shipyards with 40 drydocks for repair and new construction.

He later forayed into public service? Yes. He was twice an alderman and Louisiana Secretary of Public Safety. My dad and I were the only father/son team at the 1976 Republican National Convention. And he was Chairman of the Republican party of Louisiana.

Was he an imposing man? He was 6'4" and usually wore a cowboy hat and a big smile.

What was his style? He was honest and had a tremendous love of people.

ONE-MAN CHAMBER OF COMMERCE

Owen Edward Brennan, founder of the famed Brennan's Restaurant in New Orleans, was given a challenge. Count Arnaud, a French restaurateur told him that no Irishman could run a restaurant more elegant than a hamburger joint. From that challenge in 1946, a national landmark emerged. Ted Brennan, Owen's youngest son, reflects on the icon of the industry.

Where did Owen grow up? In the Irish Channel of New Orleans.

What jobs did he have? He was a part owner of a gas station, the bookkeeper for a candy company, a liquor salesman and the temporary manager of The Court of Two Sisters Restaurant.

When did he venture out? In 1943 my father bought the oldest saloon in America, the Old Absinthe House on Bourbon Street built in 1798. He quickly became one of the city's top hosts.

Why did he want a restaurant? After his experience with The Court of Two Sisters, his self-confidence was unwavering in the face of Count Arnaud's challenge to open his own French restaurant.

What did he name it and where was it located? Owen Brennan's French and Creole Restaurant, but people called it Owen Brennan's Vieux Carre. It was located across the street from the Old Absinthe House on the corner of Bourbon and Bienville.

What did he know about French dining? From his travels and research of its food, fine wine and impeccable service, he became the culinary renaissance man of his time, truly influencing the course of New Orleans gastronomy with top Dutch chef Paul Blange.

What accelerated the restaurant's early growth? His stubbornness and determination to put Brennan's on the national culinary map.

His greatest asset? His personality and generosity. It was once written that he would hit people over the head with his personality. He could remember everyone's name, had a heartwarming smile, incredible wit and infectious laugh. He made friends quite easily.

He was called the "Wonder Man of the New Orleans Restaurant Industry?" His quest for impeccable food and service put Brennan's on the worldwide map, almost overnight, as he charmed his way into the hearts of all who knew him.

His secret? Entertaining and befriending celebrities, including Gary Cooper, Vivien Leigh, John Wayne, Barbara Stanwyck and Walt Disney, but particularly literary favorites and media icons such as Hedda Hopper, Tennessee Williams, Leon Uris, Earl Wilson, Walter Winchell, Hank Ketcham, Lucius Beebe and Robert Ruark.

Why was he called a one-man Chamber of Commerce? After people dined at Brennan's, he often took them on tours. A master at public relations and always selling the magic of the city, my father was the founding Chairman of the New Orleans Tourist Commission.

Why is Brennan's unique? After Frances Parkinson Keyes wrote *Dinner at Antoine's*, my father revived a 19th century custom, the three-hour breakfast created by Madame Begue. He called it Breakfast at Brennan's. For this, Brennan's is world-famous.

Dishes tied to this famed breakfast? Eggs Hussarde, Turtle Soup, Grillades and Grits, Eggs Sardou and Bananas Foster - a Brennan's creation.

When did Brennan's move to Royal Street? He had a soft opening on November 1, 1955. Three days later, he died in his sleep of a massive heart attack.

His moniker? The Happy Irishman of the French Quarter.

A STOP SIGN MEANT
TAKE AN ALTERNATE ROUTE

Photo Courtesy of Erik F. Johnsen

Niels F. Johnsen saw an opportunity after World War II to pursue his lifelong dream of owning a ship. At the age of 52, his long awaited plans came true and so began the start of International Shipholding Corporation, now one of the largest fleets of United States and foreign flag vessels providing international and domestic maritime transportation services. Erik F. Johnsen, his son, talks about the man with the determined spirit.

When did your father become interested in ships?
His father and grandfather were owners of cargo carrying sailing vessels.

When did he come to America? In 1919. He had been learning the whaling business in Australia and traveled from Australia to San Francisco, New York and New Orleans where he continued to learn ocean ship agency work.

Who came up with the initial idea? During World War II, the United States constructed about 6,000 ships since the German and Japanese submarines methodically torpedoed allied merchant shipping. Congress enacted the War Ship Sales Act of 1946 to offer the remaining war built ships to commercial interests. This allowed my father and his interested friends to establish a ship owning company by buying one of these vessels.

How did he acquire the first ship? He and his friends had to come up with $580,000.

What did he name it? The S.S. GREEN WAVE.

How was business after the War? A significant rebuilding of Europe and Japan was required. Then Secretary of State, George Marshall, conceived a massive economic program, embraced by President Truman and coined The Marshall Plan to accomplish the task. Heavy shipments of aid followed, helping the United States export trade for years.

How did he accelerate the company's growth? He started very traditionally. His creative moment came when we took naval architect Jerry Goldman's design and pioneered the idea of bringing Lighter Aboard Ship (LASH) vessels into the Middle East.

What do you remember most about him?
He was always prepared to tackle adversity.

What was he known for? Sensible determination. If a goal was reachable, he put everything into making it work.

When he started, did he have a mentor? He was his own mentor since he lost his father and grandfather early. He became a ferocious reader, fluent in several languages and followed the markets very carefully.

What personal skill do you think served him best? He managed operations and cost control very well and believed there was always a way to accomplish a task.

What early products did the company transport? Food products, locomotives, cross ties to rebuild European railroads, cotton and general cargo.

How did he manage through down cycles? It was a time to make things shine because it was a time to make the market work for you. If he ever saw a stop sign, he thought that meant to take an alternate route.

What was his best advice? If somebody tells you something, always double-check it.

Your best advice? Stick to what you know!

What is your personal business philosophy? Do it right, but maintain your stance.

NECESSITY IS THE MOTHER OF INVENTION

Photo Courtesy of The Latham Corporation

James Martial "J.M." Lapeyre was 16 years old when he invented his first piece of equipment, the automated shrimp peeler. That invention was followed by over 200 others and helped to develop the Laitram Corporation, which today manufacturers Intralox modular plastic conveyor belts, Lapeyre Stairs and other Lapeyre inventions. Son Jay Lapeyre looks back at the pioneer inventor.

What kind of man was your father? Hardworking, innovative, fiercely independent and a bit wild.

What made him want to invent a shrimp-peeling machine? At that time, shrimp were being peeled by hand. J.M. had taken note of a shrimp that had been stepped on, causing the meat to be separated from the shell, and began to tinker with the idea of putting pressure on a shrimp to peel it.

What did he use? Rollers. He figured out a way to get the most meat out of all sizes of shrimp without messing the shrimp up.

What change did this create in the marketplace? It lowered retail shrimp prices and changed the way seafood was processed.

And he was just 16 years old? Yes, living on the bayou in Houma, Louisiana.

Did he invent any other shrimp devices? He created a de-veiner, a grader and other peripheral machines.

Did he finish school? He got a degree in architecture from Catholic University.

Was he always a tinkerer? Apparently so. He had over 200 patents.

What were his most noted inventions? Modular plastic conveyer belts, electro-optical printing systems for computers, digital compasses for 3-D seismic surveying and safety stairs known as Lapeyre Stairs.

What was unique about his conveyor belt? It was the first plastic modular conveyor belt and is now the world-wide standard in industrial applications.

How and why did he invent Lapeyre Stairs? He saw a workman struggling to carry a load down a steep stair on an offshore rig. To experiment, he went home, sprinkled powder on his feet, and left footprints as he walked down the stairs. Noticing he used only half the tread, he created safer, more compact stairs.

How many Lapeyre Stairs exist today? About 60,000.

What were some of his other ideas? A diesel engine, a turbine, a computer keyboard and energy-recovery devices.

Did he continue to research throughout his life? He studied and observed mechanics, electronics, physics, structures, chemistry and computers.

How did he test the products? Very rigorously. And then he hung on tight to the products that passed the tests.

What was J.M.'s view of innovation? Necessity is the mother of invention.

What were your father's strengths as a businessman? His thorough understanding of and adherence to scientific fundamentals, his ability to concentrate and his unwavering commitment to his ideas.

What was his work ethic? He was a hard worker who believed in setting a good example and often worked late into the night on his ideas.

What do you consider his best advice? Background has nothing to do with potential so it doesn't matter where you begin, but where you wind up.

MEET THE CHALLENGES

Robert L. Suggs saw an opportunity in the oil and gas industry to provide transportation for workers to and from the marshes in South Louisiana in a safe and reliable mode. Under his leadership, Petroleum Helicopters Inc. (PHI) operated the world's largest commercial helicopter fleet. Upon his death, wife Carroll Suggs became Chairman, President and CEO. She reflects on the man known as the father of the commercial helicopter industry and a true pioneer.

What was his background? Bob graduated from Texas A&M and earned a Masters in Electrical Engineering at California Institute of Technology. He worked for Humble Oil & Refining Co., a forerunner to Exxon, as a geophysical supervisor in the Far East from 1936 through 1940. During World War II, he achieved the rank of Colonel and was chief of staff of the Eastern Air Command in the Middle East. He received the Bronze Star.

What got him interested in helicopters? While serving in the Army Air Corps (now the United States Air Force), he became aware of the advancements in aviation and technology and realized this would significantly expand the opportunities in the oil and gas industry.

What was his first foray into business? In 1947, he founded Offshore Navigation Inc., a seismic company.

When and how did he establish the business? With a vision to provide safe, reliable transport for the crews working in the marshes of Southern Louisiana, he started PHI with $100 thousand, eight employees and three Bell 47 helicopters.

Was PHI founded solely to service the seismic industry? With his geophysical background and his military experience, he wanted to create an oilfield service industry which assured oilfield workers safe and reliable transportation in the swampy, mosquito-infested coastal marshes of Louisiana.

Did this change the outcome? Transport by helicopter allowed the seismic crews the ability to take multiple shots in a day and had far less of an environmental impact on the marshes.

When did he move into offshore transportation? As exploration and production grew in the Gulf, so did PHI and its fleet of helicopters.

What defined success? In 1970, PHI logged one million flight hours – equal to 200 round trips to the moon. Bob was proud of PHI's many accomplishments, especially having the largest commercial fleet of helicopters in the world that operated with a commitment to safety and excellent service.

Did he bring innovation to the helicopter industry? Bob and his team worked closely with the manufacturers to design helicopters that met the challenges of the harsh environment in which they operated. PHI was instrumental in designing modifications to address their customers' requirements.

Was offshore transportation highly regulated? Not at the time. Bob was instrumental in developing safety and training standards from which the industry grew. It has been said that anyone who flies in a helicopter today is safer because of Bob Suggs.

What other services did PHI provide? In the early 1960's and 70's, PHI transported power poles in the mountains, slung bananas across river beds and performed for NASA the first mid-air retrieval of a rocket launched space payload returning to Earth. Additionally, PHI supported many government agencies from border patrol in the Sinai Desert to National Science Foundation initiatives in Antarctica. PHI also had dedicated air medical services and maintenance divisions.

To what did he credit his success? To the ethical dedication and unconditional loyalty and skill of his employees, as well as the support of his family.

THE REAL SIZZLE: HERE AND NOW

Photo Courtesy of Randy Terrell

Ruth Fertel created the sizzling filet and with that founded the international chain of steak houses called Ruth's Chris Steak House. A decisive and determined leader, Ruth often credited her success to hard work and the waitresses who ran the business for her on a daily basis. Son Randy Fertel describes the charismatic spirit of Ruth Fertel, from her younger years in Happy Jack, Louisiana, to her legacy of building the largest upscale restaurant chain in the world.

What was Ruth's idea of perfect happiness? Being in the game and opening new restaurants.

What did she consider her greatest achievement? Winning the New Orleans Handicap Horse Race in 1977 with Tudor Tambourine, the longest shot ever to win.

It wasn't that she was the founder of an international chain of steak houses? Most people don't realize that she was the first licensed female horse trainer in Louisiana.

What supported her early growth? She was fearless, incredibly competitive and had guts.

What was her most marked business trait? Incisive intelligence when it came to anything subject to mathematical analysis.

In your opinion, what made her so successful? She was always "in the present," very focused on the person or task she was with at the time, and always there: here and now. This, to me, was the real sizzle.

In business, what was her greatest fear? As a child of the Depression, bankruptcy.

What business strategy, if any, do you think she may have wished she had perfected from the start? Franchising.

How did she view failure? Pick yourself up and go on to the next challenge.

Did you work in the kitchen? Yes, I butchered.

What do you wish she had taught you that you didn't know until you became more involved in the business? How to read a spreadsheet and that everything is sales, whether you are slinging hash or ideas.

What did she most dislike about business? That she couldn't do everything herself.

Whom did she admire? John Folse and Ella Brennan.

What did Ruth look for in employees? She looked for people who were as unstuffy as she was.

What did she consider the most overrated virtue? Patience.

Was she ever indirect? Yes, in the expression of emotions to those close to her.

Was she extravagant? Yes, in her gifts to others.

Which words or phrases did she overuse? How long has this game been going on?

What do you think she valued most in her friends? Loyalty and the ability to have a good time.

What was your mother's favorite saying? If you love what you do, you'll never work a day in your life.

How will Ruth be remembered? With a book in her hand, if she wasn't holding a deck of cards or a calculator or a shotgun or a puzzle piece or a spatula. And as a role model for the next generation of female entrepreneurs.

ALWAYS LOOKING AT THE HORIZON

Patrick F. Taylor was born in Beaumont, Texas and lived a true rags to riches story - leaving home at 16 years old, graduating from LSU in three and a half years and building one of the largest individually owned oil and gas companies in the United States. His wife, Phyllis Taylor, became CEO of Taylor Energy upon his death and remembers the man that always knew he would be his own boss.

How did Pat get into the oil business? He studied petroleum engineering at LSU.

His first job? He worked for John W. Mecom, Sr.

Was he an outdoorsman? He enjoyed everything from hunting in Africa to boat racing on the Mississippi River. His adventuresome nature began in college with rodeoing, which didn't sit well with his employer so he switched to skydiving.

Were you worried? I thought he was invincible. I even sewed one of his parachutes.

What did his boss think of him skydiving? He fired him.

Did he ever go corporate? Yes, but soon realized it wasn't a good fit. So, he formed his own company.

What was his original company? In 1974, he started Circle Bar Drilling with a silent partner, John W. Mecom, Sr. In 1979, he went on his own, founding Taylor Energy Company.

How did he get the capital for that? He came home one day and told me we were going to borrow $60 million. We were living in a small apartment so I knew the risk, but Patrick had confidence in himself and people believed he would deliver.

Did he start with a business plan? Yes, but it wasn't your typical business plan. Patrick was a true "wildcatter." His strategies were based on thorough research backed up by gut-instinct.

His greatest business asset? He was quite a negotiator and would not take no for an answer.

What moves led to growth in his early years? Patrick reassessed and then purchased under producing fields. Later, we became the first individually owned company to drill in federal waters.

How did he manage in tough economic cycles? We tightened our belts, assessed the economic situation and produced our reserves prudently.

What type of worker was Pat? He was driven to succeed and worked 24-7.

Was he intolerant? Yes, of complacency.

What type of manager was he? Hands on - involved in every aspect of his company.

How did he operate? The "acquire and operate asset management" business model.

Did he continue to innovate? In 2004, SIMBA was launched and installed in the Gulf of Mexico. This was the company's largest fixed platform.

What were his passions? First and foremost education – nothing illustrates this more than his championing the cause of educational opportunity for the youth of this nation. He spearheaded the adoption of legislation for the Taylor Plan (TOPS), a college tuition-assistance program based on merit.

His formula for success? Hard work, guts, integrity - and he felt that a little intelligence didn't hurt.

What was his most consistent state of mind? Anticipation – he was always looking at the horizon.

Pat's motto? So much to do, so little time.

CLASSIC ENTREPRENEUR,
ALWAYS MOVING THE CHEESE

Al Copeland was a young man who wanted to serve his fried chicken that many thought was too spicy. He opened a chicken joint, painted his roof red and started serving the spicy chicken. Today over 1,900 Popeye's Chicken and Biscuits outlets serve people around the world. Al Copeland, Jr., talks about his father's dreams for Popeye's and Copeland's of New Orleans, a restaurant chain expanding throughout the South.

What was life like for your father as a young boy? He was very poor; there were times he didn't have shoes and he didn't make it past the ninth grade.

What were his first jobs? He was a soda jerk first and then worked at Schwegmann's bagging groceries.

What brought him out of poverty? While at Schwegman's, there was a kid who was really fast at bagging groceries. My father asked the kid why he was working so hard and the kid told him that he was the best and would never be beat. Dad saw this as a challenge and worked hard to beat him and wanted to be the best at everything from that day forward.

Then what? My dad's brother gave him a job at a Tastee Donuts and then he opened his own Tastee Donuts franchise. He worked 18 hours a day and made $500 a week. He thought he was the richest man who ever lived.

What brought him into chicken? He noticed that the Jim's Fried Chicken across the street was open from 10 a.m. until 10 p.m. They were open for fewer hours than his business, yet they were bringing in bigger sales. He realized he was in the wrong business and opened Chicken on the Run.

Was it successful? It didn't work because there wasn't enough volume. But before he would close the doors, he decided to try selling the spicy chicken he had cooked at home.

Did people like it? Yes. He believed if he could get his chicken into your mouth three times, you were hooked.

He was that confident of the taste? He was a ge-

nius with food and had a palate that could recognize what people love to eat.

Did you like the spicy chicken? I found it too hot as a kid but ate it six days a week for seven straight years while I worked in the restaurants.

How did he get the name Popeye's? My parents went to see *The French Connection*. When Popeye Doyle appeared, Dad leaned over and said, "What do you think about calling it Popeye's?" It was the most ridiculous thing my mother had ever heard.

What makes it so special? The secret is in the batter and spice. We used to have the ingredients come to our garage at home. We would mix it there and send it to the restaurants. Today we supply the mix to Popeye's around the world.

Did Popeye's transform the industry? Yes. Today there is not one chain I can think of that doesn't carry a spicy chicken product. I think dad was way ahead of his time, pairing biscuits with chicken and red beans and rice. The biscuits themselves increased sales 20% system wide, and some stores saw profits increase 100%. That kept us on top of the game and leading the chicken industry.

Your father's favorite spot? The test kitchen.

Did he have a weakness? He kept people waiting.

What was your father's management style? Classic entrepreneur, always moving my cheese.

His best advice? Never give up. When all the chips were stacked against him, he always came out on his feet.

II. At The Helm

INVENT TO ACCOMPLISH
SOMETHING NECESSARY

Jerome Goldman studied naval architecture at the University of Michigan when he was 16 years old. Brought to New Orleans to work for Higgins Industries, he settled into the city that now solidly claims him. Goldman's designs for ships and rigs transformed the maritime and energy industries. He founded his company in the 1940's and his work continues to be used today as the true measure of innovative design.

When did you become interested in naval architecture? Growing up in the Midwest surrounded by farms.

Why naval architecture? I wanted to be able to design ships as a profession.

What was your first job? At 19 years old, I went to work for Higgins Shipyard. Twelve thousand people worked there. As the only qualified naval architect, Andrew Higgins often turned ideas over to me.

Why did you leave? The wartime business was over by then so I opened my own little office.

Any notable clients? In 1947, a California Company, now Chevron, was in the oil pioneering business and wanted to drill offshore. They first called on me to advise and design boats for offshore supply vessels, but I designed numerous other marine projects, too.

What did you give them? I designed the S44, the very first offshore mobile drilling rig. It could work in up to 20 feet of water, which was considered deep then, and became the first mobile rig in the world to drill in the open ocean. We arrived on location out of sight of land. It was 20 feet down and 20 feet above the water. When we went out to the first location and set the rig on the bottom, the tool pusher looked as if he had never been so frightened in his life. He then noticed how calm I was and said if I wasn't worried, why should he be?

Did the rig produce? Yes, it drilled many fields.

Why did you do this? Chevron engineers were capable land engineers but had no knowledge of naval architecture.

Then what did you do? The shipping business had a cost structure where it cost more to move a ton of cargo onto a ship than to sail all the way to Europe. I studied this problem and invented a new kind of ship, the All-Hatch, to move cargo more cheaply and quickly. I brought it to Delta Line, which was replacing their fleet, and their President, Captain Clark, pioneered the use of it.

And you kept inventing? Steamship companies spent zero on research. In order to make progress, I had to bring a fully developed concept to them and convince them to build it.

What was next? I developed the Lighter Aboard Ship (LASH) to load barges aboard a lighter vessel for transport. The All-Hatch became the father of containerized ships in the world and the LASH carried big floating containers weighing up to a million pounds each. These barges could be offloaded in the seaport and towed to inland locations.

You are considered a true pioneer. I'm just fortunate to have the opportunity to break new ground.

Was selling your designs easy? I spent a lot of time studying how my ships and rigs were going to be used so I sometimes ended up with more knowledge than the people I was selling to.

Define excellence. For me, it comes from a thorough knowledge of science and engineering.

Advice for entrepreneurs? Don't invent for the sake of inventing. Invent to accomplish a valuable development that will do something that is necessary and that no one yet knows how to do.

IMAGINE IF WHAT YOU LOVE TO DO
BECOMES YOUR JOB

Cosimo Matassa, grocer and musical pioneer, grew up in the French Quarter among other Italian families that had settled there. At 18, he opened the J&M Recording Studio and eventually gained credit as the developer of the "New Orleans Sound," mixing piano and horns with heavier drums, guitar, bass and vocals. He is now in the Louisiana Music Hall of Fame.

Where did you grow up? In the same neighborhood as my family's grocery store, Matassa's. We lived above the store.

What ignited your love for music? I backed into it. I was majoring in chemistry at Tulane, became disenchanted with being a chemist, and went to work for a jukebox company.

How did you start your own business? I opened an appliance and record store with Joseph Mancuso and put a room in the back for recording.

Was the recording studio an immediate hit? Little by little, people started coming in to make demos.

What jobs did you perform? I was the recording engineer and would introduce people.

When did the name change to Cosimo Recording Studio? In 1955, when we moved, we changed the name. Everyone was already calling it Cosimo.

Who was your first big client? Roy Brown with "Rocking Tonight."

What was the atmosphere inside the studio? I had an open door policy and encouraged young people to hang out there.

How did you best work? I always felt that I should be invisible. If I could be in a room and get a band to make a sound, and then go in the recording studio and get that same sound, I was doing my job.

What inspires you? A great performance, when someone can emit the emotional content of a song to the listener.

What did you look for in a singer? People who were unique and had a style and sound that you knew was their own.

What if a singer couldn't sing? I was blunt. I'd ask them if they had a waterbed because they would need a place to put their records when they didn't sell.

With whom have you worked? Mac Rebennack (Dr. John), Ray Charles, Smiley Lewis, Lee Dorsey and others.

Your most famous song? Maybe Little Richard's "Tutti Frutti."

What about Fats Domino? Dave Bartholemew found Fats playing in the Lower Ninth Ward. He was a highly unique individual with an innovative sound – that rolling, rhythmic piano playing sound.

Did you realize you were creating a new sound? There isn't really a uniform New Orleans sound, but there were bands and musicians conforming to what clients in highly-specific New Orleans neighborhoods wanted.

Your greatest strengths? Cost consciousness and no biases.

To what do you credit your success? I loved it. It was fun. Imagine if what you love to do becomes your job.

Your best advice for entrepreneurs? Coins only and bite the coins.

LIFT YOURSELF UP

Leah Chase, the Queen of Creole Cuisine, first worked at a fancy French Quarter restaurant. Harboring a desire to bring white linen tablecloths and silver flatware to the African American community, she helped develop Dooky Chase's Restaurant, and turned it into a world-renowned cooking establishment.

Where did you grow up? In Madisonville, Louisiana, but I was sent to New Orleans to live with an aunt for high school.

Tell me about your first job. It was at the Colonial Restaurant in the Quarter. I was 18 years old and had never seen the inside of a restaurant. The owner taught me how to wait tables.

What did you learn by waitressing? How to perform by not letting people down.

Did you cook? I made breakfast and sandwiches. There were three of us: Estelle was 16, Lucia was 19 and I was 18.

What was the first dish you cooked? Creole wieners and spaghetti.

What drove you to open your own business? I wanted a nice restaurant like those in the Quarter so people in the African American community could eat out.

Were you angry about the inequality in those years? The adversity makes you work harder, and bitterness destroys you.

Your in-laws already had a restaurant? My mother-in-law sold sandwiches and gumbo from this same corner where we are located today.

Were they mentors? Emily, my mother-in-law, was gutsy and a good money manager. Dooky was a lottery vendor who also loved to parade. I follow people who teach me.

What did you bring to the table? I introduced the way to set the table using silver and cloth napkins. I introduced hot meals at lunchtime. Most African Americans had no exposure to this and had to learn how to eat out.

But you spent most of your time in the kitchen? Yes. I feel like a giant in the kitchen.

How did you create your best Creole dishes? I learned about people and what they liked to eat.

Customers certainly like your gumbo z'herbes. It's become a signature dish served every Holy Thursday.

Any other signature dishes? My fried chicken.

Where do you get your continued inspiration for cooking? I read all the food magazines.

What has been the biggest key to your success? Not to focus on the money, but to focus on service. The money comes after you focus on the customer.

What do you like about having a restaurant in New Orleans? You can be a big fish in a little pond.

What motivates you? Nothing comes easily and nothing is free. You have to take risks.

You have become a premiere collector of African American art. What do you look for in a piece? Something that talks to me.

What does art teach you? That you cannot stay in your own little world.

Your motto? You have to lift yourself up.

IF A BANK IS WILLING TO FUND THE IDEA, IT'S USUALLY TOO LATE

Photographed by Paula Burch Celentano

Alden "Doc" Laborde has been inducted into Fortune's Business Hall of Fame and continues to break new ground. In 1953, as the creator of Ocean Drilling & Exploration Company (ODECO), he changed the drilling industry. As a founder of Tidewater in 1954, he created the largest offshore vessel company in the world. And in establishing Gulf Island Fabrication in 1985, he continues his iconic career of innovation and leadership.

What was your childhood like? I grew up in the small city of Marksville, Louisiana. We were lucky – we had electric lights, running water, bug screens, a phone and a radio.

Did you go to college? I went to LSU for one year and then entered the Naval Academy, graduating in 1938. After serving at sea for two years, I was transferred to the reserve because of defective vision. When World War II began, I was recalled to active duty and served for the entire war.

What are you most proud of? Developing loyalty and morale as the captain of a Destroyer in the North Atlantic. I was only 27, so I grew a beard, let my hat get a little salty and smoked a pipe to help me look a little older.

How did you begin in business? I took a job in seismology and then went to work at Kerr-McGee Oil, the company that made the first offshore discovery.

What was your first major innovation? A submersible, transportable drilling rig. At Kerr-McGee I had observed the problems of offshore drilling and realized there must be a better way to do it.

What type of reception did your idea receive? Most people turned it down, but my wife watched the kids as I hit the road and began pushing the idea to everyone.

Were you a good salesman? It was not my forté; I often wished I was more extroverted.

Who finally signed on? Murphy Oil was looking for an innovative technology that would let them compete with the big companies drilling offshore. They invested in the project and we named the company ODECO.

Does innovation always meet resistance? Yes – people usually follow the norm.

Some believe your design changed the world. Your response? Things happen.

Why did you start another company? Ten of us got together with the desire to build support vessels, which I thought were needed in the oil and gas industry.

What role did you play at Tidewater? I designed the first vessels and organized a group of investors to build and operate them.

Years later you ignited a third business, Gulf Island Fabrication? I got a call to look at a distressed platform-building facility during the industry's toughest times. With another investor, we were able to buy the company and resume operations.

What does this company do? We design and build structures for offshore drilling and production.

What are the keys to your success? Timing, taking risks and good luck. If a bank is willing to fund the idea, it's usually too late.

What lessons have you learned? Don't go into debt and always have a good strong balance sheet to survive the inevitable shortfalls that come in downward cycles.

What should every entrepreneur do? Maintain enthusiasm and grit because successful ventures take long hours and hard work.

What advice do you have for budding entrepreneurs? Family time is often sacrificed, so it helps to have the right kind of spouse.

Do you have a motto by which you do business? Maintain your character and don't take shortcuts.

BRINGING PEOPLE HAPPINESS EVERY YEAR

Blaine Kern, otherwise known as "Mister Mardi Gras," knew what he was destined to be from the time he was a boy. Now the Chairman of Blaine Kern Artists, Kern Studios, Kern Sculpture Company, Mardi Gras World and Kern International, he is the name most associated with floats, trucks, beads, doubloons and almost everything Carnival in New Orleans.

What was your first job? I started as a storyteller. My dad told incredible stories that I would repeat at school, drawing on a blackboard to illustrate them.

When did you become an artist? My father painted signs and did artwork on vaudeville theaters. I helped him during the Depression, so I learned how to paint and sculpt in his studio.

How did you venture into parades? Once when my mother was in the hospital, I painted a mural on the hospital's wall to help pay her medical bills. A doctor, Dr. La Rocca, was the Captain of the Krewe of Alla and he asked me to work on his parade.

How did that transpire into designing floats? I was building my first parade when Darwin Fenner, the Capitan of REX, sent me to Europe to see how they built floats with the idea of improving his parade.

What did you discover? I couldn't believe how beautiful they were - this was what I wanted to do.

Was anyone else building those kind of floats? No. Not even Walt Disney.

You met Walt Disney? He saw a gorilla I made and was impressed. He wanted to hire me on the spot. I turned down his offer to be an employee, but continue to do work for Disney to this day.

You opened your own company? Yes. We designed and built floats.

Did you have a business plan? Absolutely not. I'm one of the worst business people there is, but I have an imagination that never stops.

How have you changed the landscape? We created an art form for Mardi Gras that is unique.

As your company grew, what services did you add? Major event production. We also now create artistic sculpture and carnival art for clients like Disney and Universal Theme Parks. And we have Mardi Gras World where you can get a taste of Mardi Gras year-round.

What are you working on now? An entertainment center on the New Orleans riverfront featuring amphitheaters, a ferris wheel, and with Tulane, a research vessel to harness the clean, natural power of the Mississippi River.

What are your greatest achievements? I am so proud of helping to start Bacchus, but also opening Mardi Gras to everybody. So many people have now been able to enjoy the thrill of riding a float.

What do you look for in employees? Enthusiasm.

What excites you? I am always raring to go, so everything has me excited.

Where else have you produced parades? All over the world, including China.

What makes you tick? I'm a dreamer, and my dreams do come true.

Why do you love Mardi Gras? I get to bring happiness to people every year.

Your greatest business asset? My reputation as a fair and honest entrepreneur.

Any extravagances? I love art, women, culture, clothes and travel.

What do most people say when they see you? Throw me something, Mister Mardi Gras.

GOOD SERVICE WITH INTEGRITY

John Laborde became President of Tidewater Marine in 1956 after a group of ten friends came up with the idea to start an offshore vessel company. Today they are the largest offshore vessel company in the world, following the drive for oil and gas to the shores of six continents.

What was your first job? I went to law school and then went to work in the New Orleans office of Richardson Bass, an independent oil and gas company.

How did Tidewater start? Drawing on his naval academy background, my brother, Alden "Doc" Laborde had the idea of a new vessel design that would better serve the oil and gas industry because, at the time, there were no such things as offshore rigs. Companies would build a mound of clam shells and have a barge rig sit on top. Only if it was within sight of land could a barge or other vessel service it.

Who jumped on board? Two of my older brothers, as well as a few others who were interested in taking a risk in the oil field service.

What were the first vessels? Ebbtide followed by Riptide. Both were 120 foot supply boats.

What brought you to Tidewater? At the time, it was sort of a mishmash of an operation in need of some semblance of order and someone to take the helm. When it was suggested that I become full time president, Alden said, "I don't think he knows the difference between the bow and the stern, but okay."

Did you start with a business plan? No. Right after I started, I asked someone for the financial records and he said, "We don't have any." We had to develop a plan as we went.

How did you raise capital? One investor, Burch Williams, was an aggressive thinker. He had the idea of making the company a public company and raised about $500 thousand from 50 people.

What happened then? Within 15 years, we were the largest company of its kind in the world.

To what do you credit your early growth? I had a board of sophisticated people who pushed me to grow, expand and be profitable. I was willing to be aggressive, but timing was also important - and a lot of luck.

What business strategy do you wish you had perfected from the start? I wish I had gotten an MBA. I could have used that in my early years as I struggled without a financial background or experience in the boat business.

How have you created change? We set the patterns for domestic service in the Gulf of Mexico, but were not afraid to venture into the international market. Along the way, we also created a gas compression service company which in 1994, the year of my retirement, was the largest in the U.S.

Give an example of a challenge you had to work through. The industry is a very cyclical one. We experienced a downturn from 1983 to 1990. A corporate raider attacked us. Our board stuck with us and helped us make it through.

What is your business philosophy? Good equipment and good service with integrity.

What do you think contributed to the greatest successes at Tidewater? We are a very humanistic company. We had enough youth and enthusiasm to raise families while keeping our business boiling.

Reflect on your success. Leading a strong public company like Tidewater was a great departure from my life plan of practicing law in a small town.

What inspires you? I have always tried to be an achiever. I got my kicks out of doing things well.

Both you and your brother are industry icons. Our family credo is to do right and work hard.

INCENTIVES MAKE JOHNNY RUN

Ted Kritikos began as a civil engineer after serving as a paratrooper in Japan during World War II and later in Korea. With a strong desire to start his own business, he scrounged up $500 and a car, joined forces with John Owensby, and opened the inspection company Owensby & Kritikos in 1962. Today they provide inspection and testing services to the petroleum, petrochemical, maritime and offshore industries.

Where did you begin? Our first office was in half of a barbershop.

How did you fare? We didn't draw a salary for six months.

What was your role? I did most of the sales but also helped with engineering and inspection.

Did you like to sell? I believed in what I was doing. The hardest but best paying job is a salesman because you're paid by how well you do.

Were you ever told no? Of course. But I saw it as a challenge and would just turn around and go right back.

How do you handle resistance? If someone tells you it's not a good time to go into business, I would say, "Then what is a good time to go into business?"

What served as your inspiration? The opportunity to work on my own and experience the American dream.

What type of inspections did you perform? Visual radiography, magnetic particle inspection, dye penetrate, helium leak testing and many others.

Did you bring innovation to the testing? We just worked to improve the tests, build our product and make it exceptional in the industry.

How many people left your company to start other businesses? A heck of a lot and I'm pleased for them because that's what America is all about.

What is your greatest challenge? Surviving.

What do you consider your greatest achievement? Being successful in business and providing a livelihood for other people.

What other business ventures did you pursue? We started with inspection, then opened an engineering company, a company that fabricated control systems and a production management company.

What did you learn from that? People are your most important commodity.

Do you service just oil fields? We used to service primarily offshore and only about 10% chemical plants, but now we service primarily refineries and 15% offshore.

How do you recognize good employees? By promotion - put the carrot out in front of them. Incentives make Johnny run.

Does money drive entrepreneurship? Most entrepreneurs have been without a penny not once, but several times, but they took the risk and worked hard.

Define excellence. Providing a service in the best way we know how and doing it legitimately.

What is your personal motto? If you treat other people the way you want to be treated, you can't be too far off.

What advice do you have for entrepreneurs? Learn all you can about an area and pursue it until you master it.

SMALL BUSINESS GROWS
INTO BIG BUSINESS

David Oreck

Photographed by Don Young

David Oreck started the Oreck Corporation in 1963 at the age of 40 and built it into one of the leading providers of vacuum cleaners with a network of over 500 stores nationwide. A consummate entrepreneur and distribution genius, Oreck today operates a charter airline service and has just launched his newest venture, selling fragrant candles, ensuring that homes are not just clean, but filled with comforting scents.

What was life like for you as a young boy? I lived through the Depression and will never forget the despair of that time. At 17, I joined the Army and flew bombing B29 missions over Japan in World War II.

How did you begin your career? After the war, I worked in sales for the RCA wholesale distributor in New York City and eventually became the general sales manager. I sold everything from radios and phonographs to the first microwave ovens.

You witnessed a magnificent evolution. I was there when they introduced the first black-and-white TV, when Bendix invented the first automatic washing machine and for the introduction of color TV.

Did you have a mentor? General David Sarnoff, the founder of RCA and NBC, and the man who received the signal from the sinking Titanic, always inspired me.

What made you want to go out on your own? I wanted to start a business, create jobs and provide solutions. I knew that whatever I did I would have to create jobs, because if it wasn't creating jobs, it wasn't providing a solution.

How did you make a transition to vacuums? Whirlpool made an upright and was not having success. They allowed me to redesign the machine and gave me the exclusive rights to market them throughout the United States. They produced a prototype for me under the RCA Whirlpool label. I borrowed some money and hit the road.

How did you wind up in New Orleans? In 1963, the RCA distributor here was struggling and RCA wanted to know if I would be interested in taking it over. I came to this city on a beautiful December day, bought the floundering business, and turned it around from last place to first place in two years.

How did you get that golden touch? That's like someone asking, "How do you become creative?" If you have to ask...

What made your product work? The value. That's what matters – not price.

Yet money is why you grew. If you can't make a profit, you shouldn't be in business.

Do vacuums do more than clean up? Of course. They contribute to your health and well-being and protect your furniture.

What is the most important element to master in the service industry? Control your distribution so you won't be controlled by it. That and the art of marketing.

Any interesting customers? I have a picture of Johnny Carson carrying an Oreck vacuum cleaner aboard his yacht. Today, over 10 million customers use an Oreck vacuum.

What other companies did you start? A charter airline service, a Spanish electronics repair mail-order business, and one of the first master antenna companies in New York City prior to cable television.

Your view on business? This country was built on small business, and we can't forget that small business grows into big business.

Secret to your success? No one can outwork me.

MAKE A FINE BALANCE SHEET

Peter Mayer wears glasses and a bow tie to frame his happy face as he proudly points out the exposed brick wall in the expanding offices of Peter Mayer Advertising in the Central Business District. After graduating from journalism school in 1967, Mayer entered the advertising arena and now runs the largest ad agency in Louisiana.

How did you begin? After college, I sent my resume out all over the country. I got a job offer in New Orleans and began working for the *Times Picayune's* advertising department. My first boss is still my best.

What did you like about him? He spat in a spittoon.

Why did you start your own business? A lady that I worked with, Dot Cahn, told me I could do it on my own. I was scared but took the risk.

How did you secure new business? On my first account, I did it as a trade.

What was the advertising world like in the 1960's? Television was the craze.

You have a great reputation as a pitchman. What business strategy do you wish you had perfected from the start? Other ways to contract for desired profitability.

Looking back on those years, do you have any regrets? Refusing a new business opportunity.

How did you view success? A fine balance sheet and nobody unhappy.

What was your weakness in business? I was undereducated in business techniques.

How do you view failure? Not being able to make a living.

Your agency became the largest agency in the state. What did that say to you? When our agency grew to over 100 employees, it called for a celebration.

Tell me about your team. They make me look good.

How do you recognize good employees? We like one another, respect one another, challenge one another and want one another to succeed — the same way you do with your family.

What personal traits do you dislike? Procrastination and ineptitude.

What do you consider the most overrated virtue? Order.

Of what are you most proud? My sons, all three of them.

What is your greatest extravagance? Exotic food and things.

What is the quality you most like in a person? Trustworthiness.

Which words or phrases do you most overuse? Schmuck.

What other professions inspire you? Architecture and law.

If you were to die and come back as a person or a thing, what would it be? A bull in a pasture in Montana. You know, that's the punchline of a dirty joke.

What do you most value in your friends? The old shoe feeling of comfort.

What is your favorite saying? *C'est la vie.*

YOU'VE GOT TO HAVE FAITH

Tom Benson grew up on the edge of the Ninth Ward before enlisting in World War II at 17 years of age. Rising through the ranks in the automobile industry, he began to purchase dealerships, banks to finance car purchases, and real estate. A successful entrepreneur, Benson was approached in 1985 by the Louisiana governor to purchase the New Orleans Saints, turning the hometown boy into a regional hero.

Your first job? I delivered newspapers as a boy.

How did you get your start? I attended Loyola and started working at Mike Persia Chevrolet in accounting. Mike taught me a great deal, and I was good at financials. Later I was given an opportunity to manage a dealership in San Antonio, Texas, and I eventually bought it.

To what do you credit your early growth? When I started in the automobile industry, banks were being used to finance car purchases and repairs. I soon realized it would be more cost-effective to bring all of that external financing in-house, so I bought a small bank and took the middleman out.

Did you continue to grow? Yes, to 35 car dealerships and we purchased more banks as well as real estate. Today we employ nearly 2,000 people.

How did you handle challenges? You don't enjoy losing, but you find a way not to lose again by working at it until it's successful.

How did you move into professional sports? I heard that the Saints were going to be sold to an outside interest in Jacksonville, Florida. A local group tried to purchase them, but it fell through, so Governor Edwards tried to put a group together. When he asked me to come meet the group, I discovered I was the group. The rest is history.

What did you know about professional football? Nothing, but I always believed in hiring good people. Jim Finks, the renowned sports executive, served as president and general manager. He was my teacher.

What makes the Saints an economic engine? Our entire organization has done an amazing job of making a real difference in our community. The Saints are rivaled by very few professional teams when it comes to our fans. That projects to the world that New Orleans is alive and well! People see that and want to be a part of what is happening in our great city.

What's next? We purchased the local Fox affiliate, an office tower and real estate near the Superdome. We've brought Smart Cars to the region. We are on the cusp of building new Mercedes Benz facilites in New Orleans and San Antonio as well as refurbishing the Chevrolet dealerships in both cities.

And you secured another Super Bowl? Yes. Super Bowl XLVII in 2013. I take great pride in promoting our city to the other NFL owners.

The most challenging time for you? My wife died, followed by my son and then my daughter. I later lost my second wife. It was tragic and taught me that you must have faith.

Define excellence. When you set out to accomplish something and you work toward a goal and then you do it. The key is to enjoy what you do.

What happens when the Saints play well? We work a little harder, walk a little faster and think a little harder.

What do the Saints mean to New Orleans? They're a part of the social fabric that makes up our city. Generations have grown up with the Saints. The bond between our team and our fans is truly unique.

BE THE BEST AT WHAT YOU DO

James R. "Jim Bob" Moffett was a young football player in Texas when a legendary coach took him under his wing to teach him lessons on leadership. Capitalizing on those lessons, in 1969 he co-founded McMoRan Oil & Gas and today runs Freeport McMoRan Copper & Gold, the largest publicly traded copper producer in the world.

Who inspired you to start a business? I played football under Coach Darrell Royal at the University of Texas. Coach Royal taught me about leadership, not with arrogance but with confidence. He would say, "If you have to tell people who the boss is, you shouldn't be the boss."

Did you have a mentor in the industry? Ken McWilliams was a senior geologist who taught me how to have a big-picture approach to things. For example, he showed me how to look at the regional impact of an area versus a single project.

Why did you establish your company? I didn't want to waste an opportunity to generate assets and then have someone else take over my assets.

How did you secure capital? Mack Rankin came in to work with us and from that we met a lot of people who could finance oil and gas production.

Which activities led to growth? We had some early discoveries and a solid belief that we could find oil and gas with a small team.

Was the first discovery exciting? There is nothing like having results as an inventor or explorer.

How important was timing? Very. We were lucky that we were finding things at the same time that oil and gas prices were escalating.

What accelerated your growth? Oscar Wyatt had just come up with the idea of selling natural gas intrastate and we got a contract with him. We produced a well with a discovery of 90 BCF of gas at 2,000/MCF.

Was gas more profitable than oil for you? Yes.

Natural gas was the commodity that built our company.

Did it slow down? No. The next big discovery was in the Gulf of Mexico. Transco became our partner. Gas went from $2 to $9. That's how we were able to purchase Freeport Minerals in 1981. Freeport came to us because they were stagnant. Fortunately, from that we found Main Pass 299, a major sulphur and oil deposit in the Gulf of Mexico.

What has been your most significant discovery? Grasberg, Indonesia, the biggest discovery of copper and gold ever found.

What do you consider your greatest achievement? Picking a subject like geology – I liked it and it liked me – and the leadership that I took from football.

What is your strength? I am a scientist with an ability to communicate, which makes me more multi-faceted.

Define excellence. Being the best at what you do.

What inspires you? Public education, where melting pots of kids are offered the key to go from rags to riches.

Define success. Reaching a point in life when you can help others be successful.

What advice do you have for budding entrepreneurs? You can't be afraid of hard work. You can have the greatest job in the world, but if you're not willing to work hard, you will never be excellent.

Mignon Faget, the preeminent jewelry designer, is a true daughter of New Orleans. Since 1969, people all over the world have been wearing her designs, yet she steadfastly maintains her dedication to loyal customers. With her unique ability to pair jewelry with fashion, the designer has just introduced another collection from her New Orleans studio and workshop.

When did you begin to design? I began to design as a child – it was very natural to wrap leaves and twigs found in our garden into a costume. While other girls played with paper dolls, I would draw out dresses for my mother to sew.

What prompted your designs? Professor Robin Fields taught Design in Nature at Newcomb College, where I received my BFA. We would pick a botanical form and elevate it into a series of drawings - into art. I found my passion.

Did you begin with jewelry? No, with clothing. First as a child and then in the late 60's with my own clothing collections.

Your first designs? I was married with three children and I went back to school. My instructor told me that I had a flare for design so I created a border pattern for a garment and decided to show it. Two New Orleans stores, Town & Country and D.H. Holmes, bought it.

Then what? I was still operating at home. I would draft a pattern, cut out the pieces, bundles them up and drive to different seamstresses to have them sewn into finished garments. As much as I loved to design, I was never patient enough to sew.

What brought you to jewelry? I had a huge collection of seashells I used as accessories to my clothing. I became fascinated with the transition from the real shell to sterling silver. This is the genesis of my career in jewelry.

How did you manage operations? My ideas were sophisticated, but the operation was not. The studio accidentally turned into a retail shop and I had no idea how to run a retail shop. I found someone with all the talents that I didn't have, Charlotte Norman. Charlotte managed people very well, she was no-nonsense and ran my operations for over 30 years.

How did you fashion your shop? It was the beginning of the boutique era, with avant-garde SoHo boutiques that I loved. I wanted it to be personal and to be in touch with my customer, from the mailman to the chairman of the gala.

First location? I rented half a cottage in the Riverbend. I wanted it to stand out as special so New Orleans artist Tim Trapolin painted a French countryside mural on the entire facade.

Did you have a mentor? Several. My old friend Jean Seidenberg pushed me along with technical advice and encouragement and Larry Merrigan, president of the Bank of New Orleans, believed in my business potential even before I believed in myself.

Business acumen? Stubborn and determined.

What is your greatest challenge? Time.

What inspires the collection names? Names are usually inspired by the source. For example I studied botany and learned of plants that arm themselves with thorns and spikes – it is called passive armament. The next collection was Armament.

What else did you learn in botany? Nature has all the answers. Plants are a perfect source for jewelry design.

What is success? Passing on my excitement over a design to the person who will wear it.

Business philosophy? Originality in my work, while expressing my love for New Orleans.

IN A STATE OF GRACE

Quint Davis, President of Festival Productions, Inc., is best known as the producer and director of the New Orleans Jazz & Heritage Festival. Jazz Fest, the largest outdoor musical festival in the world, consists of 12 stages and has an annual attendance of more than 400,000.

How did you begin? I was studying Ethnomusicology and working in the Hogan Jazz Archives at Tulane.

What assets did you bring to the job? A knowledge of music and culture.

What did your early years consist of? I became a road manager, stage manager, tour manager and production manager.

Were the road trips exhilarating or exhausting? Both. We once did 44 concerts in 42 nights, including two countries in one night.

What was your best road trip? Taking B.B. King to Africa for his very first time in 1973.

Who was your mentor? George Wein, creator of the Newport Jazz Festival in 1954. This became a model for all outdoor festivals.

What did he teach you? How to construct and maintain, and the bottom line in relation to artistic structure.

Do you still seek his advice? All the time.

Why? I move in the here and now, but he sees where an issue will end up. It's been a wonderful, lifelong partnership.

What was your most important obstacle? I had to learn to recognize the sound of business. That's the sound of money hitting the table. Until you can learn to recognize that sound, you're just in a loud storm of conversation.

What do you like better, producing or directing? Producing. You can think something up and make it happen.

Were you able to innovate? Our multi-stage systems with over 5,000 musicians are pretty unique. We were also the first to put gospel choirs from a church in a secular event.

What is one of your favorite cultural successes? Convincing the Mardi Gras Indians to parade for the first time in 1970.

Why is music so important in New Orleans? Our city has a talent pool as great as anywhere on Earth for traditional American music. Our music is like food for the locals – they must have it to make life work.

What motivates you? Acceptance by the public for what we do.

What keeps you up at night? Everything.

When you hit a brick wall, what do you do? Re-evaluate and keep going.

How can the city better market its creative industries? If you want to succeed, you need to master the economics of creativity because something is important only if it has longevity.

What is the greatest challenge you face each year? Rain.

What is the least fun part of your job? People looking for free tickets after so many people have worked an entire year to put on this world-class event.

Since Jazz Fest turned 40, how do you feel? We're in a state of grace.

DON'T CONFUSE CONCEPTUAL WITH OPERATIONAL EXCELLENCE

Alton Doody was once a university professor with a knack for success. In 1972, his pioneering research on the changing structure of post-war retailing afforded clients such as Wal-Mart and Target the designs needed to lay out the stores for maximum profitability. Assisting clients in the retail, automotive, funeral home and restaurant industries, Doody turns traditional business ideas upside down.

How did you start your career? I received my Ph.D. from Ohio State and then taught there. I directed the MBA program in the late 1960's.

What early research did you conduct on retailing? I was able to document the rapid emergence of mass merchandising stores.

What motivated you then? The satisfaction of clarifying fundamental trends for executives who were perplexed by the rapid change that was taking place in the structure and economics of distribution. I started with consumer goods, manufacturers, wholesalers and retailers.

Does it excite you that your work was transformational? Yes, looking back over a forty year span, it is interesting to think about the fundamental changes in business practices, especially at the retail level, that have come about as a result of my company's work.

What did early success give you? As we grew, we were able to better identify trends and process these into strategic plans for our clients.

How did you manage through harder economic times? The key to business is to stick to a disciplined growth plan so that your overhead can withstand the ups and downs of business volume. Fortunately, we did this reasonably well. Of course, there were times when volume and profits were not in sync.

How did you handle stress? Youth! Most of us were in our 30's and 40's when we found ourselves working 60-70 hours a week, sometimes more, and traveling all over the world. We were old enough and experienced enough to know what we were doing, but our energy levels were still very high.

How did you reward the achievement of your employees? Above average compensation, generous expense accounts, worldwide travel opportunities and the satisfaction of doing work that was widely recognized as important to our clients.

What formal training do you wish you had? Additional mathematics and computer skills. My partners made up for my deficiencies, though.

When are you most creative? When I consult. Knowledge, creativity and solid research are the basis for formulating great strategies.

How do you avoid failure? Don't confuse conceptual excellence with operational excellence.

What's the difference? There is an old saying that goes something like: "A mediocre plan, brilliantly executed, will be successful." In my experience, a brilliant concept, poorly executed, will fail.

Define excellence. Substantive, measurable increases in sales and profits for our clients.

How do you feel about the future? Extremely optimistic! Technological invention, management creativity and entrepreneurial breakthroughs will contribute to dramatic productivity opportunities in the future.

What business philosophy do you adhere to most often? Peter Drucker once said, you should concentrate on the 20% of the things that produce 80% of the results. Do those with excellence, and the rest not at all!

PRIVATE ENTERPRISE WITH A PUBLIC PURPOSE

Photographed by Jeff Strout

Darryl Berger had a vision for the French Quarter riverfront. It had been disconnected from the people of New Orleans for many generations, so when the old Jax Brewery became available for purchase in 1982, he and his partners secured it. After developing a plan to reconnect the site to the river and ignite economic development, the Berger Company created a unique shopping center and other mixed uses that brought commercial life and public use back to the river's edge of the Vieux Carré, the crown jewel of the city.

Your first job? My dad was in the retail jewelry business and I worked the counter.

What did you study? History.

What got you interested in development? I grew up understanding borrowing and lending and went to law school. I loved it but I never intended to be a lawyer. I always liked finance and real estate.

What was your first project? I was 23, and my partner was 28. We had the opportunity to buy the Delta Towers, an old style building that was an apartment hotel. We were too young to know how easily we could go broke if we made a mistake!

When was this? 1972.

What was the landscape like? The city was vibrant and poised for growth. Moon Landrieu was mayor, Joe Canizaro was developing Poydras Street, high rise buildings were being built, oil and the Port were doing well and the Superdome had been announced.

How did you move to the riverfront? In 1982, Jax Brewery became available through a bankruptcy, and we grabbed it. We purchased it within 48 hours.

Had the brewery closed? It had gone into bankruptcy seven years earlier. Much of the historic brewhouse was destroyed and the entire site was totally abandoned.

What kind of riverfront access existed then? The Riverfront as a public place was essentially non-existent. Only the Moonwalk penetrated the private barriers governed by the Dock Board and other agencies.

How did you proceed? We put a masterplan in place which envisioned the site within the context of the Vieux Carré and its historic waterfront. We worked with public groups and private citizens and convinced the Corps of Engineers to create openings in their new floodwall at the location of historic streets. We had a responsibility and opportunity to create a game changer in Jax since it was a six-block piece of property along the Vieux Carré riverfront.

Your goal? To be stewards of the Jax Brewery. The goal was to be a private enterprise with a public purpose.

The results? We preserved historic gems, the Henry Howard Warehouse, the Brewhouse and the oldest buildings on the site, the Sugar Sheds. We restored the original street grid to the river, repoening Toulouse, Wilkenson, and St. Louis Streets.

What else created the success? In 1975, Wilber and Bill Dow put the Natchez Steamboat at the Riverfront. That was a breakthrough for the river and the start of the ultimate realization of public use and enjoyment of the area.

What is success to you? Being truly satisfied with your effort.

Advice to entrepreneurs? If entrepreneurship is creative thinking and creative actions that make a difference, there's no place like New Orleans. Although we're not a "money center," we're the Garden of Eden for entrepreneuship. There may be other places to make more money, but the final byproduct of entrepreneurship is not money, it's success.

KNOW THE FACTS AND BE DISCIPLINED

To: Justin Herzey
From: PC Havens

8-19-10

Good Luck!

Prentiss "P.C." Havens worked in the seismic business before venturing out on his own. In 1975, he created Seismic Exchange, Inc. (SEI), a seismic data marketing company that cornered the market by reselling existing data and acquired ownership of seismic data in singnificant areas of oil and gas explorations. SEI is one of the largest owners in the country of seismic data, which is a vital research tool for the oil industry.

How did you discover this line of work? When I was 20 my father passed away, so I needed to help support my family. I was hired for a job planting geophones on a seismic crew for Delta Exploration. Later I recorded instrument data from a truck.

What did you discover? Eventually I was able to learn every job on the seismic crew field work, and it taught me what it takes to make it all come together.

How was seismic information collected then? Crews would lay down seismic cable, plant geophones into mud, detonate a charge and receive a seismic reading of the designated area.

Where would the crews explore? Water, land, marsh and swamp. We used the first marsh buggy Andrew Cheramie ever made.

How is seismic data used? Geophysicists and geologists interpret it for oil and gas exploration.

What was the competition like? Very secretive. We stayed in hotels 20 miles away to avoid seismic scouts and maintained confidentiality for our job and clients.

What did you do next? I accepted a job with Geophysical Trade Service. Dr. Sam Taylor had ideas about reprocessing older data and transcribing it to magnetic tape. We reprocessed data from all over.

After 20 years, you started your own business. Why? I began to think about the opportunity and better ways to serve the oil and gas industry.

How was your business model different? The word "exchange" implies what we were doing by marketing seismic data owned by oil companies and leasing it to clients. This was the premise on which the company was formed.

Tell me about your early years? We had a one-room office with little overhead and worked long days, including Saturdays and Sundays, following church, to be ready on Monday.

Were you confident of your success? I had a good feeling that we would make it. Within months I could envision the possibilities for success.

What led to growth? We found an innovative way to fund a costly seismic survey by combining companies into what we called a group shoot. Following, we were able to market the seismic data to other companies that did not originally participate.

Where are you now? We own over 1.8 million linear miles of domestic proprietary 2-D seismic data and over 25,000 square miles of domestic proprietary 3-D seismic data located in the lower 48 states and the Gulf of Mexico.

Did you expand your services? Some of the oil companies had to contend with storage of their data, so we started warehousing data.

Are there still new frontiers? Seismic has moved from paper to analog tape and now to digital at a rapid pace. I am anxious to learn the next phase.

Advice for entrepreneurs? Know the facts and do your homework. Discipline is essential and hard work is an imperative component for success.

Your business philosophy? Hard work, right alongside the team.

Paul Prudhomme, better known as Chef Paul, propelled the distinctive cuisine of Louisiana into the international spotlight. Now he not only cooks up a great meal at K-Paul's Louisiana Kitchen™, but he also owns and operates Chef Paul Prudhomme's Magic Seasoning Blends™, which are distributed nationwide and in other countries throughout the world.

What inspired your love of cooking? My Mother taught me how to cook using the freshest ingredients. I can't take credit; I just did what she told me.

What is your style? I am the youngest of 13 children, so I'd say adventurous.

What motivated you to start a restaurant? I wanted to do one thing – cook to make people's dinner better.

What was your formula? I had a gift for flavor. I could put spices on something and it was just better.

How did you begin? I opened Big Daddy O's Patio. I had four restaurants that failed, and then I opened K-Paul's Louisiana Kitchen™ in 1979.

What was the response to K-Paul's? Terrific. I had 72 seats, which were always filled, and I did all the cooking myself.

What was your first product outside of the restaurant? Cajun Magic.

How did you market it? A salesman who sold kitchen equipment asked me to put it in a bottle so that he could sell it out of his car. I had to switch to a box so that the color of the seasoning didn't change.

How do you find your ingredients? I travel all over the world to learn about other herbs and spices.

When you travel, do you cook? I take cooking lessons from chefs from other cultures when I travel.

What else do you sell? Seasoned and smoked andouille and tasso, nine cookbooks and six cooking videos, two of which were at the top of the Billboard's chart for 53 consecutive weeks.

And now you manufacture? I have a very large plant which produces custom blends, bulk sizes and contract packing for other food companies.

Any new products? Salt-free and sugar-free seasonings, Salmon Magic and Barbeque Magic are delicious, and our product development team and R & D kitchen can also create flavor profiles or duplicate existing ones.

How do you manage through down cycles? Bad times can be good when they bring you back to who you are. As they always say, "Go back to the basics."

How do you approach your work? Every day I push myself to do better or create something better which will add pleasure to other people's lives.

To what do you equate your success? Hard work and determination to be able to afford people the opportunity to enjoy great food at home or in the restaurants around the country that we service.

Is cooking an art? Not necessarily. It's a feeling.

What do you consider one of your greatest achievements? Feeding the American troops on bases around the world.

What is the source of your inspiration? A desire for people to have spice in their lives.

MAKE PEOPLE COMFORTABLE

Phyllis Jordan opened a small coffee shop in 1978 to bring comfort and coffee to people in New Orleans. By discovering beans from around the world and roasting her own coffee in small batches, PJ's Coffee and Tea Company grew into one of the country's premier coffee chains. PJ's now has over 40 stores and continues to serve as the neighborhood anchor in cities across America.

How did you begin? I was a social worker and director of the state agency for runaway children in Des Moines, Iowa.

So why did you leave that? Society didn't offer much help to the teenaged kids, so I left and went to work for a record store.

Any other interesting jobs? I was the hostess in a truck stop in Iowa.

What made you open a coffee shop? There was a store in Des Moines that sold coffee products like grinders, tea balls and the like. I liked that coffee was a social thing. When I moved here, I opened a store and created the tag line: Coffee, Tea and All The Paraphernalia for the Rituals of Friendship.

Was the store an immediate success? The store was a little early to market. Coffee shops had not yet begun to appear like they have today. I could see that customers wanted a place to sit, so I spent $75 to purchase a table and four chairs. As tables filled, I added more.

What atmosphere were you trying to create? Organic hominess. If my mother, a mid-Westerner who loved classical music, was comfortable, most everyone else could be.

Why were the walls pink? Everyone looks good in pink.

What motivated you? Daily returns. I bagged groceries in my younger years and loved reading the receipt of my sales in black and white at the end of the day.

What moves helped accelerate your growth? I traded with a designer all of the iced coffee he could drink for a new logo. And in 1982, I bought my first coffee roaster, a big American-made clunker that I had to assemble by hand.

Did you ever consider food? People always wanted that, but I wanted the consumer to think of PJ's when they thought about coffee.

When did you decide to franchise? By 1988, finance and operations were locked down with two very capable people. I discovered that I liked change and growth, so I added franchising.

What do you now know that you wish you had perfected from the start? How important systems are.

Where did you find your coffee? Indonesia, Tanzania, Jamaica, Nicaragua and Ethiopia, the motherland of coffee where conditions are so perfect that it's essentially organic.

Did you become a taster? Yes, and I spit in the gaboon, but it wasn't easy to learn to make the noise.

Why did you sell PJ's? I had become the first female president of the Specialty Coffee Association of America, I had traveled to exotic and amazing places, so how lucky could a girl get? It was time.

What did you love the most? All of the kids who worked at the stores. I wish I had a photo album of all of them.

Do you miss PJ's? I miss making people as comfortable as possible.

MACHINERY, MORE EXCITING THAN A WHEELBARROW

David Guidry, founder of Guico Machine Works, was a tradesman in the oil field when he envisioned the opportunity of owning a machine shop. Today that original 1,800-square-foot shop, founded in 1982, is 58,000 square feet, making well heads, tubing hangers and flanged products to help energy companies provide oil to the world.

Where did you first begin? I was a Cajun in Palmetto, Louisiana, a rural area outside of Lafayette – all four of my grandparents spoke French. We were just country people.

Was there a family business? We had a small farm and raised our own cattle. My dad taught us business from an early age and entrepreneurship was always around.

In what way was entrepreneurship promoted? Calves were given to each of us to care for until the live stock auction. Daddy would make us do everything for the cattle and then we would bring the check to the bank with him.

What made you interested in a machine shop? One time we found an overturned wheelbarrow. My grandfather, Poppee, who was born in 1887 in Palmetto, yelled at us to get away from the wheelbarrow since we didn't know anything about machinery. I wanted to learn.

When did you leave your life in the country? I went to trade school and then got a job in the oil field.

Did you ever work with heavy machinery? The biggest machine I had seen was a tractor. When I went into an oil field and saw the machinery, my eyes were opened.

Did the machinery excite you? Yes, my brother was a machinist for Brown & Root and I told him we should open a machine shop.

What was your first step? I read several books on how to put a business plan together and wrote one up.

How did you secure capital? Seventeen banks rejected me. Finally, a bank in Dallas gave me an SBA loan with 22% interest.

Were your early years a success? We opened the doors to our machine shop in 1982. I was 24 and my brother John was 31. We had machinery that was a lot more exciting than that wheelbarrow. By 1983 there was positive cash flow.

Have you been through hard times? In 1986, our bank failed, the oil fields dried up, and the space shuttle blew up with Martin Marietta who was a customer. Green order sheets turned to blue for hold then pink for cancel.

What did you do? I took out a map to look for industrial cities north of here and picked Philadelphia because it was the cheapest round trip ticket I could find. There I found Honeywell, and they sent me some quotes. Next thing I knew, I fell into the motherload.

What lessons did you learn? That I had a national product but had to build up our workforce to a higher standard. Those two passions are still alive in me today.

What is your market advantage? Developing specialty valves.

Have you continued to grow? We've had growth and improvements in technology. We've developed new product lines and do business internationally.

What is your mission statement? We are dedicated to continued quality improvement.

What do you think Poppee would say today? "We've come a long way from Palmetto."

BE THE NEW KID
ON THE BLOCK

Bobby Savoie founded a small consulting company in 1986 to sell engineering services related to software that he had developed as an industrial engineer. Soon, Integrated Resources Group (IRG) was thriving and merged with Science and Engineering Associates. Savoie ran the company for many years and knows what it means to be the new kid on the block.

What was IRG? Integrated Resources Group was the technology company I started in 1986 after I designed a couple of pieces of software for licensing nuclear power plants.

How old were you? I was 28, and just a Cajun from down the bayou – I didn't know what I didn't know.

Describe the start-up phase? At first it was ups and downs of feast or famine, but no overhead. Next thing I knew I had 15 employees.

What ignited your growth? Commercial nuclear power started going downhill, so we looked at the nuclear market and decided on defense programs. The transition took two years, and we almost went broke but we ultimately won contracts from the Department of Defense, Department of Energy and NASA.

To do what? Nuclear safety, non-proliferation and radioisotopes.

So you have performed classified work? Yes.

What was the key to your success? We outworked everybody and produced quality work. If the work quality isn't there, you have nothing.

What was your greatest asset? We could sell ice cubes to Eskimos but we could also deliver the work we promised.

Were you the head salesman? Yes, I sold most of our contracts. These are very technical sales. In 1987, we won the restarting contract for the Rancho Seco nuclear plant and in 1990 for the high-level nuclear waste program.

What are you most proud of? I take great pride in the fact that we hired 1,000 employees who ultimately became employee owners.

Did it work? Absolutely, although we made every mistake you could make about shares. We got it right by using the employee ownership institute of Dr. Bob Beyster, CEO of Science Applications International Corporation.

How do you manage through hard economic times? Persistence and never giving up. Plus working on my own. Since 1986 I have not received a paycheck from someone else.

What business strategy do you wish you had perfected from the start? How to deal with resistance from competitors as the new kids on the block. Entrenched bureaucracies and large companies impeded our growth.

What challenged you? The bigger you become, the more of a threat you are to others.

What was your best asset? Never giving up and never being complacent.

What is your most marked attribute? Determination. I always felt like I had something important to do in life.

When are you most creative? When my mind is relaxed, usually at 2 a.m.

What is your latest accomplishment? It took me 27 years to get my Ph.D., but I did it.

What advice do you have for budding entrepreneurs? Life isn't dictated by how hard you get knocked down, it's how you get up and keep going.

PUT SOME MUSCLE BEHIND IT

George Shinn was a young boy in the small town of Kannapolis, North Carolina when his father unexpectedly died. Enrolling in a business school, he soon discovered the secrets of success through reading. Eventually, he bought that school, built Rutledge College into one of the most successful collection of business colleges in the country and became the youngest person ever to receive the Horatio Alger award for distinguished Americans. These accomplishments led Shinn to bring the business of NBA basketball to New Orleans.

What was life like for you as a child? My father died of a stroke when I was eight and my mom and I lived on welfare.

Did you stay in school? I had a mom who would never give up on me and who dreamed that I would graduate from high school. I had the distinct honor of graduating 232nd out of a class of 232.

What was your first job after high school? I was a laborer who lifted bolts of cloth at Cannon cotton mills. I started to have back problems since I'm a small guy, so hoping for a better job, I enrolled in a small town business school. That business school changed my whole life. For the first time in my life, I read books cover to cover. I began to agree with my mom that I could do anything I wanted to.

What happened next? I had no money to pay for school, but they asked us if we had friends who they could talk to about coming to the school. I told them I could help recruit, but that they would have to pay me. They had four recruiters and hired me as a student recruiter. Soon I had sold more than the four others combined. Two years later I owned the school and built the largest chain of private business schools in the country.

Did you start with a business plan? I started with a dream and then I learned through all the books I read.

Who mentored you along the way? Norman Vincent Peale, author of *The Power of Positive Thinking*, helped me most.

What brought you to professional sports? I decided at a young age that I wanted a sports team. After I hosted two exhibition games to test the market, David Stern cracked a door. The rest is history.

What is your greatest achievement? Being awarded an NBA expansion team. There were eleven cities trying to get a franchise. When we pitched, I spoke from my heart and we wound up being chosen first though ranked dead last.

What is your strength in business? My faith and my ability to motivate and fire people up, to get them to rise up from where they are and get better.

What do you look for in employees? Enthusiasm. Obviously you want them trained or qualified, but people excited about life are ready to take on the world.

Define excellence. Being the best you can be for your customer.

When are you most creative? I am not an inventor, but an innovator. We have one of the best franchises in all of sports because we always look for new ideas, improve upon them and give the customers what they want.

What do the Hornets mean to New Orleans? A social impact, an economic impact and a community impact.

What is your best advice? Dream big and put some muscle behind it.

DISCOVER TO MAKE A BETTER WORLD

Victor Castellón grew up in Cuba but came to the United States for school. His parents escaped from Cuba in the hull of a boat carrying the Bay of Pigs prisoners that had been arranged by President John F. Kennedy. Castellón celebrated the American dream by pursuing and succeeding at several ventures, including VitaRx and his latest innovation involving DNA.

Is it hard to believe that your life could have turned out very differently if your parents had remained in Cuba? I feel so lucky to be in America with my wife and children.

You were educated in the United States? Yes, I wanted to be a vet but chose pharmacy school instead.

Then what happened? I met some consultants at the beginning of the biotech revolution who needed an entity to deliver boitech's managed care. The company was called VitaRx.

And VitaRx was your national launch pad? Yes, we became a biotech specialty distribution and logistics firm that in essence merged the medical billing concept with the pharmacy concept.

You began with a single pharmacy? Yes.

What kind of growth did you experience? We went from sales of $600 per day to $210 thousand per day and from two to 200 employees in three years. It was 24/7.

What was the most challenging aspect of the accelerated growth? Accounts receivable.

Did you have a mentor? Felix Ciolino and Stuart Farber.

What do you look for in a pharmacist? A good one can deal with crisis management and handle people well.

How did you reward good employees? Bonuses.

What happened to VitaRx? We sold it to McKesson, a Fortune 25 company.

What venture followed? One of my customers couldn't pay me. When I asked him what assets he had, he said some Black Angus cows. I took 20 cows and bought a farm. My grandfather had been in the cattle business in Cuba and I was always curious about it.

But you did more than raise cattle? Yes, I started reading about DNA. In Australia, which has a highly agrarian economy, researchers had discovered the "taste" gene and the "tenderness" gene in cattle. I went Down Under and licensed the exclusive rights to those genes.

Then what? We transformed the cattle industry in the United States and eventually sold it to Pfizer in 2008.

Looking back, what is most critical in a start-up phase? Financial flexibility.

What is your business philosophy? You may have a great idea, and you may have drive, but you have to find good people. It's all about the people.

What inspires you? Discovery and its application to making a better world.

What are you working on now? My work in DNA continues, only this time I am exploring the possibility of venturing to the human side.

Define excellence. The Japanese have a saying called *wabi* that basically means perfection is the sum of all imperfections. To me, excellence is the sum of all of my successes and my mistakes.

GET UP, BRUSH YOURSELF OFF, AND GO BACK AT IT

John E. Koerner was selling boats as a young man, inspired by his fondness for fishing. As his business grew, he began to look for other business opportunities. A stagnant soda company named Barq's Root Beer became the perfect play, and in 1976 he reignited a brand that has once again become a household name.

How did you begin? With a law degree but I didn't like law so I sold boats.

Who did you work for? Clearview Marine. We did well, and I eventually bought the company.

How did you find Barq's? Ernst & Ernst brought it to me.

Did you start with a business plan? Yes, and we stuck to it for 15 years.

What was the state of the company? It was a stagnant third-generation family business in a plant from the dark ages.

What did you do to turn it around? We introduced much better business practices and used a strategy of consumer pull and distribution push.

How important is distribution? It's key – if your product is unavailable, no one can buy it.

What was your biggest hurdle? Credibility. This was a brand that had been in decline for many years.

To what do you credit your company's success? We worked hard to create a stimulating and rewarding environment, financially and emotionally, with minimal internal politics – the way a company should be run.

What was the greatest challenge to selling the product? Getting the marketplace to understand it was going to be a new Barq's.

Did you focus a lot on marketing? Yes. We had an in-house marketing team that could respond quickly to current events. Our best campaigns revolved around things like the collapse of the Soviet Union. We knew how to target our market and image the message, providing the skeleton to build the flesh of the brand.

What made Barq's work? The bottling company had value in the eyes of the bank and was the bankable piece. But trademark and atrophied distribution system were the diamonds in the rough.

Did you add any products to the line? Just the opposite. There had been lime Barq's, grape Barq's, orange Barq's and red Barq's, but we had to focus the brand. Some years later we added Diet-Barq's.

Define excellence. Making sure every detail is buttoned up.

Define success. A journey, not an end point. As soon as you succeed at one thing, you raise the bar and go for the next thing.

To what do you attribute your growth? Tenacity and learning how not to stay too long in a situation that needs to be abandoned.

What is your favorite New Orleans pastime? Talking to the characters.

Your advice to budding entrepreneurs? I don't know anyone who came right out of the box without a flop or two, so don't be afraid to fail. Get up, brush yourself off and go back at it.

CREATE VALUE

Roger Ogden was the student body president at LSU when he formulated his goal to one day become governor of Louisiana and dedicate his life to public service. But in 1975, on the strong counsel of his mentor and a natural affinity for value creation, Roger embarked on a career of real estate development upon which he built a platform for social entrepreneurship and giving back to the community.

How did you get started? With two nickels. And, truthfully, I am exaggerating, it was one nickel.

You went to law school? Yes, Tulane at the time, I still wanted to be governor.

Did you have a mentor? I interned in the U.S. Senate for Russell Long and he taught me that successful business people could leverage their effectiveness to help more people and make a broader difference than is possible in elective office.

When did you first engage in a business? In high school, I conned my dad into buying a corner lot that was for sale near my high school. When he prematurely died, title was transferred to me complete with an existing mortgage greater than the value of the property. This was my entrée into commercial real estate development because there was no net value to this land, it needed to be redeveloped.

What did you do with the corner lot? I cold called the CEO of Kroger in Cincinnati and told him I thought he needed a new super store at this location. Surprisingly, he took my call and I introduced myself as a young man contemplating getting into commercial real estate. I shared my vision for a new Kroger. He put a store on the lot. Next, I paired the Kroger Anchor lease with a Piccadilly Cafeteria Anchor lease and connecting shops to create a viable community shopping center development.

Where were you working? My office was a renovated walk-in closet off my bedroom since I couldn't afford a stand-alone office.

What led to growth along the way? I pulled in a partner, Jimmy Maurin, a then participating CPA.

Over the next ten years, we developed, or acquired and redeveloped 35 shopping centers.

What did you bring to the marketplace? A "new mousetrap" so to speak. We built higher end upscale neighborhood and community shopping centers in top notch suburban locations. A niche that no one else was doing. Most were developing non-descript "strip" centers or very large regional malls on the outskirts of suburban areas.

Then what? Then the economy of Louisiana went to hell in a hand basket. The oil patch dried up and the banks were in even worse shape. Over the next ten years, we were no longer creating value, we were trying to save our tails.

How did you adjust through the challenging times? We acquired Stirling Associates and implemented third-party real estate services that, as renamed Stirling Properties, we are synonymous with today. We changed our mission to include management, acquired a residential brokerage firm and recapitalized with a pure equity investor. We saved the company, the portfolio and our entire team.

Of what are you most proud? During the challenging times, we never let a single person go.

Your greatest strength? Adaptability, exemplified by a second career focused on our city, teaming with Darryl Berger on hotel and retail development in the Riverfront, CBD and Arts/Warehouse district.

What inspires you? Envisioning what others may not see, then working to make that vision a reality. Accomplishing that vision as a part of a team, rather than as a Lone Ranger, is the most gratifying of all.

THE ENEMY OF GOOD IS BETTER

Rich Ashman, Ph.D., holds over 15 implant patents and is a leading researcher on bone mechanics and orthopedic implants. He invented the TSRH Crosslink and Spinal Implant Systems, medical devices that became implant standards and are now used to save lives in spinal cord injuries and other spinal related conditions such as scoliosis.

Where did you learn about inventing devices? I was always interested in developing technical systems, but became more interested in medical device design during my Master's Degree in Mechanical Engineering at California Institute of Technology.

What brought you to New Orleans? When I was at Cal. Tech., it seemed many people were going to work for military or aerospace contractors. I was interested in medical applications so I came to New Orleans for Tulane's biomedical engineering program.

Why did you pursue the spine? While at Tulane, I researchered spine related disorders with Dr. Andrew King from Children's Hospital. We felt that advances could be made to existing spinal implants.

How did you come up with your invention? After mechanically analyzing existing spine implant systems, we looked for ways to improve on their limitations. Our first device was a cross brace used to lock two spinal rods together so that they better share the loads.

Has your work changed the landscape for spinal patients? Our implant system, and similar systems, along with other advances in spinal surgery have significantly improved surgical outcome and have reduced rehabilitation time after spine surgery.

The work is life-altering. It's evolutionary, not revolutionary.

To what do you attribute your success? I was lucky to be working in a field I enjoyed and was lucky to be in the right place at the right time.

As you invented these devices, you became the head of research for an orthopedic children's hospital. Is this a natural step? I worked with several orthopedic surgeons at Texas Scottish Rite Hospital to develop the use of these implants. The hospital is a leader in treating kids with orthopedic conditions such as scoliosis, clubfoot, hand disorders, hip disorders and limb length differences. My work was perfect for their mission, but I was also directing a much more diverse research effort.

And then? I moved back to New Orleans and formed a biomedical engineering consultancy, providing design and analysis counsel to medical implant manufacturers.

How does FDA approval work for devices? There are two paths for FDA clearance of devices. One is similar to drugs and can be long and costly. The other allows a more direct clearance if similar medical devices already exist.

What else have you worked on? Orthopedic implants for small bone fractures, a urological catheter and other urology products.

What happened to them? We sold the urological products to a leading medical technology company. For the small bone implants, we formed a company in New Orleans to design and market them.

Do you align with partners as you invent products? Yes. It's similar to other start ups. We first develop some basic products, apply for patents and FDA clearance, work out a business plan, find angel investors and approach the venture capital funds, while working to bring our products to market.

Do tough economic cycles hinder innovation? As times get tough, I take bigger risks.

Your mantra? The enemy of good is better.

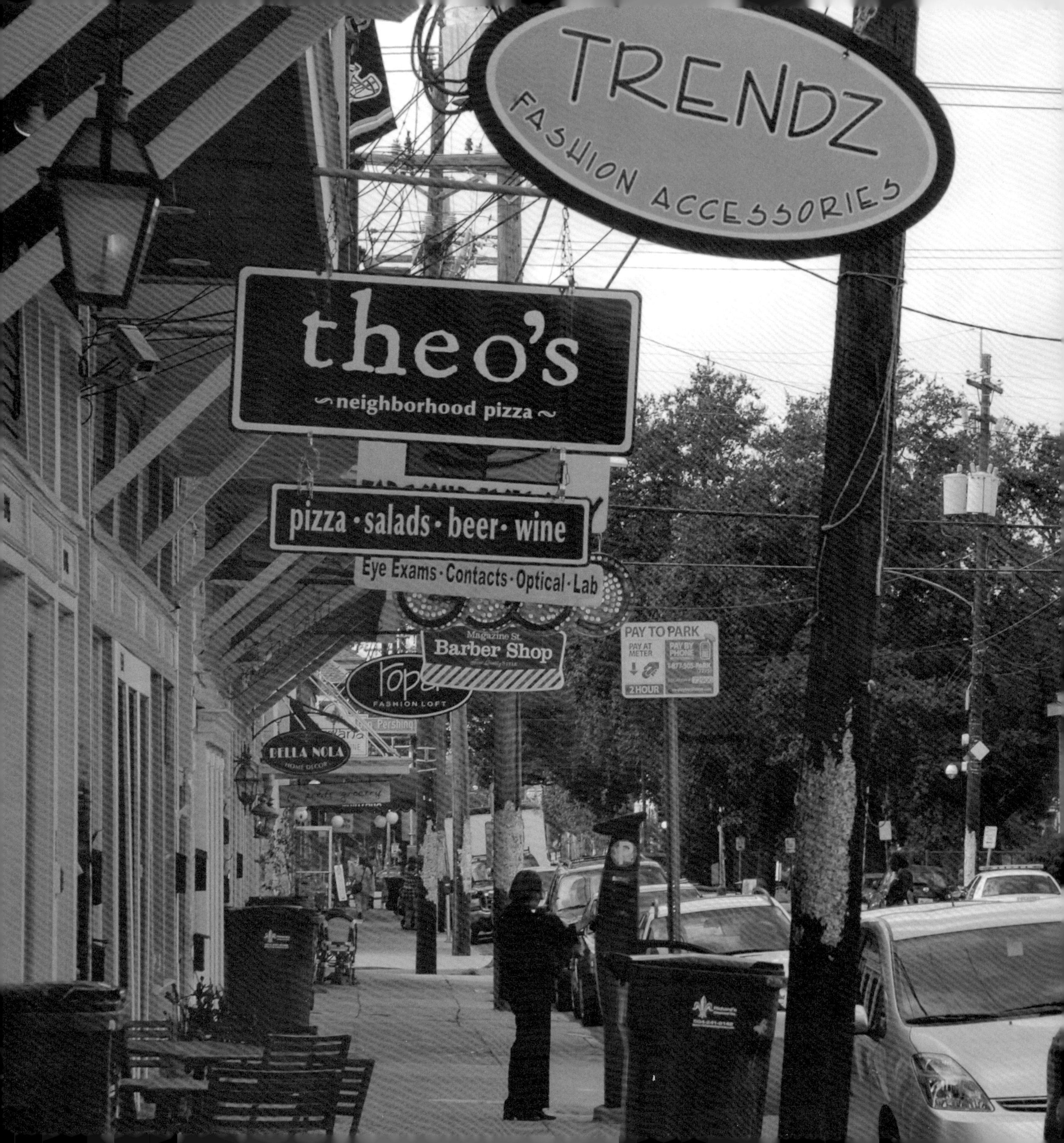

TRENDZ
FASHION ACCESSORIES

theo's
~ neighborhood pizza ~

pizza · salads · beer · wine

Eye Exams · Contacts · Optical · Lab

Magazine St.
Barber Shop

Rope
FASHION LOFT

Pershing

BELLA NOLA
HOME DECOR

PAY TO PARK
PAY AT
METER
2 HOUR

III. On The Horizon

DON'T CONFUSE EFFORT WITH RESULTS

Jimmy Treuting started in the corporate market but had a keen eye for the development of technology. Launching Communiqué, he quickly built the Gulf South's largest and most profitable internet service provider, maintaining a client base of over 10,000 small to medium size business users. In 1997, Verio, a national Internet service provider, purchased Communiqué.

What was the greatest challenge of your early-stage development? Like all start up ventures, funding was paramount to sustaining life long enough to succeed.

What did that teach you? That you can't grow a company based on outside investment because it might not be there when you need it. So grow your company rationally and based on what you can fund internally and only use outside money to help plan your growth.

How did you build your reputation as an operator? I've always run operations with a sales mentality, focusing on what makes a product easier to care for and sell. This dictated the internal workings of the company. Simplify, focus, communicate and sell a good product that fills a need. Give great service to your customer. Sounds simple, and it is.

Do you enjoy managing other people? Yes. Leading a team with a common and measurable goal is what I love to do.

What is the hardest part of running a large corporation? Finding talented people to form your team is difficult; you need to find people who match your business DNA.

Are systems important? Systems are vital to the information and communications focus. Understanding what's happening and communicating where you're headed are made efficient through the use of internal systems.

What has been the key to your success? Forming a great team and NOT doing everyone's job for them.

How do you handle a client who does not have the same level of technical awareness as you or your company? You MUST communicate to them on the level they are comfortable with, not on the level you are comfortable with. Success usually follows the company that can do that.

What motivates you? It is an unbelievable feeling and the ultimate challenge to run your own business in which success or failure depends on what you do and what you've built.

How much of your success comes from the fact that you worked at a large corporation before you became an entrepreneur? Understanding how the big boys make it work, understanding what was good and bad about that, gave me an advantage over peers or other executives that started as entrepreneurs only. I draw from that experience to manage my own company.

Your weakness? I'm unbelievably impatient, and I rely on my memory too much.

What do you consider the most overrated virtue? Effort.

What business strategy do you wish you had perfected from the start? Growth – I should have gotten bigger quicker.

What is your most marked characteristic? Being very direct.

What is your motto? Don't confuse effort with results.

DELIVER THE SWEET LIFE

Joel Dondis is as creative about food as an artist hovering over his canvas. His catering company, Joel's, quickly became known as a different type of catering experience. Expanding on that success, he opened several restaurants, including the city's first high-end dessert eatery, Sucré, in 2007.

At what age did you begin to cook? I was in my parents' kitchen when I was eight years old.

Did you know it was your passion? My sixth-grade science project was a soufflé.

Did you cook outside of your home? Yes, I had the opportunity to work in the kitchen of a friend of my father. I was picking turtle meat.

Did he encourage your aspirations to cook? Not exactly, he used the tough love approach to see how serious I was. I had to earn his respect.

Where did you receive formal training? The Culinary Institute of America and Europe for three years.

With such a love of food, why catering? It was a wide-open space in New Orleans and was the type of food that I wanted to present in the marketplace.

What were the market conditions? Very old-fashioned. In the early 90's, catered food was not up to the same creativity as in other cities.

The competition was light? The barriers to entry were very low.

How did you begin? With $5,000 and a Honda Civic Hatchback.

What lesson did you learn? Do a detailed financial plan before you begin.

Your strength? Conceptualizing the food.

How long does that take? I sketch and draw designs and can spend months on development of flavors and food pairings.

You have stores and restaurants. Are the operations similar? Retail is so much tougher than restaurants. You have to make the food, then package, merchandise, message and ship.

What do you know now that you wish you had perfected from the start? Good communication skills.

Let's talk desserts. How is Sucré different? Everything we create is made in-house in small batches and crafted from the finest ingredients available, often inspired from local, homegrown flavors.

How many products do you sell? 120 core products in four categories: Macaroons, Chocolates, Confections and Gelato. We offer seasonal products six times a year.

Who handles quality control? The whole team.

Is your online store producing revenue? Over 10% of our sales come from the Internet and the number keeps growing.

Do you still take lessons? It's never too late to learn! I take any opportunity I can from our four chefs and, as I travel, I'm always learning new techniques.

What is your style? Classical techniques using local ingredients.

To what do you equate your success? If you deliver warm and gracious customer service, all else falls into place.

Mission? To deliver the sweet life.

Harold Clarke was a rising couturier in New York City in 1994 when he brought his Fashion Institute of Technology training and exquisite line of ball gowns and evening wear to a city that loves to dress up. Today, his gowns can be seen in his showroom on Canal Street, in the windows of the Ritz Carlton, on exhibit in stately museums and draping the shoulders of glamorous women around the world.

When did you come to America? I came from Jamaica in 1969.

What got you interested in fashion? My grandmother sewed. She had diabetes and was losing her sight, so I would guide the fabric through the machine for her as she sewed.

What was your first job designing? I was 14 and had a friend who was a tailor. One day I saw him with a new shirt and asked him where he got it. He told me he made it and said that he could teach me how to make one. That is when the light bulb went off, and I realized that I could make this a business.

And from there? My friend said he could get me an apprenticeship, but the rest was up to me.

Define haute couture. Craftsmanship. Every dress is custom made as if I'm constructing a building. You need a proper foundation.

Who were the earliest believers in your work? My wife, while I mortgaged our house, and a New York benefactor who rented me a space at a generous rate in Soho, New York.

When did you realize you had made it? During my first showing at The Gallery of Wearable Art. I made more money that day than I had made in one year at my day job in a hospital.

What stimulated your early development? Nancy Reagan dressed fabulously and the ladies in New York followed suit. This helped me a great deal because they came to me for the private parties.

How does the inspiration for a design come to you? First I look at my client, then I listen to where she's going, and then I sketch to reflect the images of what she needs.

What is a satisfied customer? Clients who feel pretty and feminine in their new dress and therefore very confident about what they're wearing.

What has been your most successful business strategy? In designing, you have to keep evolving.

Noteworthy clients? I have designed for some of the finest ladies in New Orleans, but also Vanna White, Linda Evans, Delta Burke, Patti Labelle, Cameron Manheim, Mary Wilson and Urma Thomas. My dresses are also featured in in the Lifetime Original Movie, "Nora Roberts' Tribute."

Why New Orleans? When I lived in New York, I met Louis Armstrong. That was my first connection. Years later, when I came down for a client, I took a streetcar ride down St. Charles Avenue, and I was inspired to stay.

So you stayed? Yes. That was it. Some of my best experiences have happened here.

What has been one of your best experiences? I was chosen to do a Rita Hayworth retrospective by a French bridal magazine. The mass international promotion led to a meeting with a New Orleans bride who needed her entire bridal party fitted. Once we arrived, the rest is history.

What is your motto? You have one life to live and you have to do the best you can to make it worth it.

LOOK FOR THE BEND IN THE ROAD

Todd Hornbeck recognized the potential that deepwater production created for the offshore service vessel industry and started Hornbeck Offshore Services in 1997. Today, the publicly traded company owns and operates the second largest fleet of "new generation" offshore service vessels in the United States.

How old were you when you started? I was 28 years old.

Did you have a business plan? Yes.

What created this opportunity? The onset of deepwater offshore drilling by oil companies was a bend in the road that established service vessel companies did not react to.

How did you begin? I went to potential customers and asked what type of vessels they would need for deepwater drilling. They told me that larger vessels with more capacity and "dynamic positioning" technology were needed.

What is considered deepwater? Deepwater is 1,000 to 3,000 feet and ultra-deepwater is now up to 10,000 feet.

What do you transport in offshore vessels? Fuel, drilling fluids, drill pipe, equipment, people and anything else needed as part of the drilling campaign. Our boats provide an umbilical cord to the rig.

What innovations have you introduced? We have a proprietary design for most of our fleet. We recently introduced the HOS 370, which is the largest supply vessel in the world and the only vessel in the world certified as a supply vessel, a construction vessel and a tanker.

What excites you about the advances of your vessels? Our ability to transport ever increasing amounts of cargo and to transfer in a faster and safer manner.

How big are your vessels? We have three general classes of vessels, the first of which range from 200 feet to 265 feet in length. Our HOS 370's are 370 feet in length, and we just launched a 435 foot long construction vessel that cost $115 million to build.

Why did you take the company public? I needed capital to build more ships and scale to survive the cycles. Today, we have a fleet of 85 ships and many more in design or under construction.

Who was your greatest teacher? My father, a shrimper and oysterman who started a company of supply vessels that later merged with Tidewater, the largest owner of offshore vessels in the world. He is beyond tough. He is a hardworking, honest pioneer in our industry.

What is your best asset in business? Understanding the industry and what it needs in order to offer quality and safety of service.

What is the key to your success? Hiring the right people and giving them a piece of the action.

What do you wish you had perfected from the start? Financials – I would have grown even faster.

Faster than this? Yes, I was conservative in my capital aggressiveness.

Define success. Creating an iconic company that is revered as the thought leader in the industry, while pioneering operating solutions.

What challenges you? Winning the war. Every day the competition is out there to replace us.

DON'T STEP IN YOUR OWN GUM

Mark Samuels played at fraternity parties in a band called "The Urinals" before realizing his true dream: to succeed in the music business. Working nights and weekends to discover all aspects of the industry, he launched Basin Street Records in 1997. The label now serves as the Motown of New Orleans and home for some of the city's most noted musicians, including Jon Cleary, Jason Marsalis, Kermit Ruffins, Irvin Mayfield, Theresa Anderson, Dr. Michael White, Jeremy Davenport and Henry Butler.

What was the label's first project? It was in 1997, the recording of Kermit Ruffins' The Barbecue Swingers Live in front of a packed house at Tipitina's in New Orleans.

Describe your label. New Orleans-based jazz, blues, funk, rock and R&B.

Your artists are impressive. Yes, they have won Billboard Music Awards, have been nominated for a Grammy and WC Handy Blues Awards, have had a number one CD hit on the national jazz radio charts and had several CDs on the top ten radio charts.

What do you look for in an artist? Someone that I can listen to everyday.

Do you work in the recording studios? I don't like to shape the raw material. I prefer to just market and promote music that I love.

Who are your clients? The artists.

What has contributed most to your success? People respect that I work hard for them – and I deplore laziness.

Is it really that hard to represent these great artists? It takes vision, patience, perseverance and long hours. The hardest part is finding balance.

How do you view failure? If you learn from it and improve, then it wasn't.

What is your greatest achievement? Raising three children (ages six, eight and ten at the time) after my late wife died. I'm not sure they would agree though.

Your strength? My desire to see these artists succeed and train others to do the same.

Your weakness? What has become a love of clutter.

What business strategy do you wish you had perfected from the start? Evaluating expenses more carefully.

What do you fear? Going out of business.

Have you come across scoundrels in the business? My mom taught me to keep my mouth shut if I didn't have anything nice to say.

What is the quality you most like in an artist that you want to sign? Honesty.

What profession inspires you? Teaching.

What do you most value in friends? Their Facebook status.

If you were to die and come back as a person or a thing, what would it be? Sting.

Any regrets? It would be nice to have the first million back.

What is your greatest extravagance? I don't feel that I live extravagantly but also realize that 99% of the world would gladly trade places with me.

Favorite quote? Don't step in your own gum.

Jonathan Ferrara had a desire to give a voice to the creative mind, the creative process and the artists working to manifest their ideas. He opened Jonathan Ferrara Gallery in the Arts District in 1998 to showcase art that is edgy but still has the aesthetic qualities to work within a home. He credits his success to scrappiness and an eye for picking creative talent, which New Orleans has in abundance.

Is the business of art unique? Yes. We don't provide food or shelter. Our product feeds the soul.

Do you look for art that has broad-based appeal? At the gallery level, the quality of art should be a given. After that, the message, beauty and purpose comes into focus.

How do you operate? It's not rocket science: take care of the needs of the artists who supply the product and the collectors who purchase the product – and take great care of your employees in the middle.

What is your sales approach? I focus on the people who have a desire for my product and appreciate and understand art. Then, if they express interest, I follow up relentlessly (sometimes for months) until the sale is consummated.

What makes you different? I have an unusual amount of energy, I work non-stop, think way outside the box and dedicate a lot of my time to helping artists.

What business strategy do you wish you had perfected from the start? I wish that I actually had one from the start.

You didn't start the gallery with a business plan? No. I have gone the organic route with a lot of wings, prayers and hard work. And, of course, an eye for great art.

How do you innovate? I learn from my mistakes - replicate what works and don't replicate what doesn't. I have learned to trust my ideas and instincts when it comes to creative concepts and business opportunities, and I always, always follow through.

Your greatest achievement? Never giving up on my dream of being an artist and gallery owner while living a creative life.

What challenges you the most? Patience.

What inspires you? Art, artists, the creative process and those who believe in both.

How do you define excellence? Knowing what you have to do, and getting it done.

Greatest regret? None. If opportunity is a Mack truck speeding down the road, I'm standing in the middle of the road saying, "Hit me."

What is your business philosophy? Fake it 'til you make it, and work your butt off.

Lessons learned? The simple ones: Have your doors open when you say you will; do it and think ahead; anticipate what will happen next.

How do you recognize the achievement of your employees? I try to praise my employees as much as I can, give them license to think for themselves and recognize them in front of clients so they feel appreciated.

Motto? A creative dictatorship is better than a creative democracy.

Has success changed anything in your life? Success is relative. I take my success and reinvest it, doing bigger, better, crazier creative things that will have an even greater impact.

BE FLEXIBLE IN YOUR BUSINESS MODEL

Kenneth Purcell founded iSeatz, the only Louisiana company to land on *Inc Magazine's* list of the 500 fastest-growing companies two years in a row. Established in 1999, it has evolved into the industry's leading provider of customizable travel and entertainment booking solutions. iSeatz offers global leaders instant access to over 200 thousand service and product providers. After years of perseverance, Purcell finds iSeatz hitting its stride and growing with rapid success.

When I met you, you were living and working in the same room and washing your hair with soap. How does it feel to have made it to the top? Well, I was living with my parents but definitely spending too much time at the office! Where we are feels great, but I realize that every day is a new day and each day can bring success or failure.

Did you start with a business plan? Yes, but it continues to evolve as we respond to the market's needs.

What does iSeatz do? We develop the merchandising strategy for the "travel check out line." In a nutshell, we stock the impulse item shelves for websites like Delta, MasterCard and Air France/KLM.

How? By applying our vision, market intelligence and award winning technology platform to compliment our partners' needs. Our incredibly flexible software has become the industry benchmark.

Your sales strategy? Referrals actually, but it wasn't always that way. It started with making thousands of cold-calls. Now, with clients like Delta-Northwest Airlines, Air Canada, Air France/KLM, Citigroup and MasterCard, it's a bit of a downhill run in terms of new client acquisition.

Explain the evolution of your business? We were first a tool that allowed hotel concierges to book on-line restaurant reservations very efficiently. Then, we expanded to tickets, tours, hotel bookings and rental car reservations. I can imagine that we may also get into retail-related item sales. We moved from focusing on a B2C strategy to being totally B2B.

How did your software design change? We built the first product to book online reservations and evolved it to include tickets, tours and other items. From there I could see that there was clearly an underserved middle-market gap for customized solutions and began to expand the technology and services we offered to meet the industry's needs.

Lessons learned? To be laser-focused on our goal and to be flexible in the path to arrive there.

What business strategy do you wish you had perfected from the start? The art of building a world-class team; it often takes different kinds of people to start a company than those who truly know how to run a business.

Where is the growth in your industry? We see tremendous opportunity domestically and abroad. We are constantly growing our supply base, improving our delivery systems and increasing our scalability.

Keys to success? Surrounding myself with people who are passionate about our business and have done something like this before. My team is on fire with a renewed passion and commitment to making contributions to the rebuilding of New Orleans.

What keeps you up at night? That my shareholders, team and their families are counting on me.

Why New Orleans? There is a quality of life here that can't be achieved anywhere else.

What keeps your blood pumping? My drive to be so much more than what we are.

Matt Wisdom has a passion for the digital effects industry. In 2000, alongside his brother Andy, Matt saw a market opportunity in the 3-D image arena and pounced, creating Turbo-Squid, now the largest online marketplace for 3-D images. Architects, global news organizations, artists, musicians and companies worldwide buy and sell models, plug-ins and surrounding technologies through TurboSquid.

What got you interested in the business? When I was a kid in the 1980's, I wrote primitive graphics software. After seeing *Jurassic Park* in 1993, I was absolutely smitten.

What does your company do for your clients? For suppliers, they now have potential buyers from all over the world. For the buyers, they can concentrate on the creative side because we supply the fundamentals and foundation for their project.

Did you secure venture capital funding as you were starting to grow the company? Yes, we received funding from Advantage Capital, Intel and Kodak, which accelerated our growth.

Can anyone sell his or her artwork or digital music on your site? Yes and they do, or they try to.

Do you solicit artists? No, they find us. We have artists submitting work from all over the world.

What are some of your favorite images? I love characters. Artists make crazy stuff like flying cupid demons that look cute but could tear your head off. Imagination is truly the only limit these days.

Do you have images of space and the depths of the oceans? Yes, and images of spacecraft such as shuttles, and technical images of military aircraft and equipment. We have almost everything.

What is happening in the world of images? 3-D is seeing a convergence where it can be displayed everywhere.

A convergence of media? Yes, television, film, Internet, software, mobile devices, video games and the like.

Where do you put your energies? Since we have such a large inventory of images, we stay focused on the selling side.

Is the video game business a significant market for you? Very much so.

Has New Orleans helped or hurt your brand? This city is a blessing because we can attract world-class talent and retain them.

How are you driving your company? I look more at the rudder and less at trimming the sails.

What has you excited about the future? The transition to 3-D online. Google's new browser already allows people to see web pages in 3-D.

What about television? That's next. TV in general will be switching to 3-D.

But will we need glasses to watch 3-D TV? Yes.

Advice to budding entrepreneurs? Indulge your denial.

What lessons have you learned? Prove your sales before you raise your costs.

What should every image seeker know? Click it, buy it.

YOU GOTTA HAVE THAT DOG IN YOU

From left: Roy Markham, Irvin Mayfield

Ron Markham and Irvin Mayfield, college roommates with energy, determination and a desire to develop a business around something they revered, have a contagious love of jazz. Embracing that affection, they created the New Orleans Jazz Orchestra in 2002 to nurture the living, breathing art form of jazz. Markham explains the business of jazz.

What is the New Orleans Jazz Orchestra? We are a performing arts institution dedicated to creating and presenting authentic, engaging and transformative jazz experiences for audiences far and wide.

What made you do this? Irvin and I started playing as teens and recognized the deficit in jazz institutions. There wasn't a model in existence, and we thought such a model was worthy of creation.

Did you start with a business plan? No. We just decided that Irvin would be the artist, and I would figure out the rest.

Which activities led to growth along the way? Listening to elders, observation and continuous hard work.

What do you consider your greatest achievement? Creating a jazz model when I was emphatically told it was impossible.

What has been particularly challenging? Getting people to realize the value of New Orleans culture. Especially jazz.

What business strategy do you wish you had perfected from the start? Putting the right people on the team.

What have you learned from your growth? That there's plenty more to learn.

Toughest part of operating? Creating a sustainable model with jazz at the center.

What inspires you? People telling me what's not possible.

How do you define excellence? The perpetual search for inexorable greatness.

When are you most creative? Under duress.

How do you recognize the achievement of your employees? By encouraging them to reward themselves.

Which words or phrases do you most overuse? Maximize, sustainable, excellence.

What formal training do you wish you had? Formal training can be highly overrated.

What did you learn from the greatest failure of your life? That life is full of ignominies and soon to come failures.

What would you do differently if you could start over? I would not be so cautious.

How do you push through obstacles? You gotta have that dog in you.

What important lessons have you learned? You can accomplish anything as long as you don't care who gets credit for it. People who are not as advanced as you are sometimes capable of the best advice. When everyone gets scared, get greedy. When everybody gets greedy, get scared.

What's cool about jazz? It's the only art form dependent on the individual and the collective.

Favorite hangout? Wednesdays at Irvin Mayfield's Jazz Playhouse.

Arnold Baker traveled to the township of Alexandria in Johannesburg, South Africa and was introduced to a community redevelopment strategy involving concrete ready-mix plants. These economic engines were to generate jobs and help create and support new business in highly-impoverished neighborhoods. Back in the states, he established Baker Ready Mix in 2003 on that same spirit of change and progress.

What was your first job? I was 11 years-old and borrowed $45 from my dad to buy a lawnmower. I paid back every penny in less than a month. This was my first lesson in entrepreneurship.

Did work inspire you? The spirit of business inspires me. Growing up I saw businessmen on TV but didn't know one. At 18, my mom bought me business cards and an attaché case – I thought I was the coolest guy on campus.

How did you begin? On crutches at a mall about to graduate from high school, I realized that I was not going to be a pro- athlete. I had an epiphany about working there, so I went to the office and asked for a marketing internship. They said no, but I went back every week for three months until they hired me. My desk was a fold- up card table next to the breakroom.

What did you do? I implemented marketing and advertising for malls but trained in every department they would allow me to. I found my love in redevelopment strategies for urban malls and in discovering the economic impact that successful efforts had on communities.

Why did you start your own business? I was blessed in business and wanted to share the experience I gained, make a difference and set an example for younger generations to exceed.

You saw the benefits of a concrete plant. What did your analysis show? That multinational interests control the concrete industry and that to have a chance at success, each plant would need to be grounded in a local, grassroots commitment.

How did you secure funding? I went to a very conservative bank, they said no. This beat me up, but it bullet-proofed me. Each time they rejected me, I went back with an improved plan. Finally I got it.

Then what? We opened, experienced a merciless on flop but re-emerged with new vision and strength. Once a month, I would spend three to five days at a different plant or manufacturer learning best practices to adopt and bad practices to avoid.

How was Baker Ready Mix different? It was the most technologically advanced plant in the state when we opened, raising the bar in concrete innovation.

What is your best asset? You can trust my word. You may not like it, but you can trust it.

What do you wish you had known from the start? Knowledge and experience can be bought.

How do you recognize achievement? Growing and promoting from within.

Best advice? Commit to getting smarter as a company or prepare to sell.

What do you fear? The day I retire will be the day I experience fear.

Lessons learned? I will go out of my way to do business with good people. It's worth the personal investment to help good people achieve success.

Your philosophy? Thou shall not bear false witness against your product, your person or your business. If someone lies in this company and is caught, they're gone.

Chris Schultz is the geek's geek, and has launched Voodoo Ventures, LaunchPad and Flat-sourcing, to name a few of his businesses. LaunchPad started in 2009 as the first co-working venture in the city, a shared space for start ups and a center for sharing costs, talent, skills, resources and ideas. Together with Barre Tanguis and Will Donaldson, Schultz has pulled together engineers, designers and other entrepreneurs to grow an ecosystem of supporters.

When did you become a software geek? The first time I used a computer.

What was your first job? I launched an online bachelor party business, all very tasteful I might add, for people interested in going to Vegas.

What drives you? I love the $0 - $500 thousand growth phase of a company.

Why the challenging start-up phase? It is certainly the most risky, arguably the toughest, but personally the most rewarding. For me, it's what comes naturally.

What is the biggest hindrance to success in early development? Cash flow. You should never be undercapitalized.

What do you like least in business? Managing others – I'd prefer they manage themselves.

What business strategy do you wish you had perfected from the start? Engaging your customers before, during and after you have built your product. I learned this after I spent two years building a product nobody wanted.

How do you view failure? There is a big difference between failing and being a failure. I've been an entrepreneur for ten years and endured many more failures than successes, but you learn so much more through failure.

What did you least enjoy during those times? Nightly bowls of Ramen soup, but that's also the beauty of bootstrapping.

What do you look for in an employee? I have no patience with employees, clients, partners or anyone who is not an honest, trustworthy and ethical person.

What is the trait you most need to change about yourself? My tendency towards distraction. I tend to get excited by new, bright, shiny objects and can neglect things that need my attention.

Whom do you admire? I consider Thomas Edison my business hero.

What is your greatest extravagance? I have to have nice equipment to do my work.

What is your pet peeve? I hate buzzwords like "out of the box," "thought leader" and "change agent." When I hear myself using them, I banish them from my dictum.

What other profession inspires you? Musicians. The dedication and depth of craft to produce a great song is inspiring.

What profession would you least like to pursue? Wall Street banker.

What is your most marked characteristic? Every Friday I take an entrepreneur to lunch.

What is the first thing you advise? Doing business with friends is tough.

What is your favorite saying? "Let us run with perseverance the race that is set before us" (Hebrews 12:1). It signifies the importance of living life to the fullest and always giving your best, no matter what twists and turns life may take.

TAKE A GAMBLE

Jon Sherman has a passion for wallpaper. After hearing about a West Coast wallpaper entrepreneur whose brother was burning the company's equipment and inventory, he jumped. Frozen in time, the company owned hand-screened motifs from the 60's and 70's that Sherman has brought back in style with Flavor Paper, founded in 2003.

What do you do? We custom make hand-screened wallpaper and fabric.

Did you start with a business plan? I did a little research to see if it could work.

Recent successes? We were on the cover of *Dwell Magazine*.

What has been your smartest business to date? Taking a huge gamble on wallpaper.

Would you say you reignited the wallpaper industry? Absolutely.

When are you most creative? When I'm not overstressed.

What inspires you? Global travel. I visit museums, I look at nature and architecture and I visit a lot of art exhibits. That's where I get my ideas about patterns, and then I apply something unique to the pattern.

When I first saw your scratch-and-sniff wallpaper, it brought back so many memories. The reception to it has been incredible.

Who buys it? Well, we just did a huge order for a candy store.

What's new? Every spring we add between seven and ten patterns. Soon we will start a new "Flavor of the Month."

What are your strengths in business? Operations and marketing.

What challenges you the most? Keeping up with government taxes. There seems to be no easy way to deal with any of it.

Define excellence. Stepping above the norm by leaps and bounds.

In business, what do you fear? Trends.

Why? Because wallpaper has gone through such ups and downs that people could become fickle and say it's out.

That's a challenge. Yes, but I use it to stay ahead of the game.

Best asset? My creative side has been well received. People wonder what ad agency we use because we're so popular.

What is your current state of mind? Frustration with my contractor as I try to open another office in New York.

What phrase do you most overuse? We don't keep anything in stock.

If you could change one thing, what would it be? More sleep.

Where do you see creativity? In Josh, our print master, and in street art.

What formal training do you wish you had? More graphic design.

How do you feel about the future? It's looking great.

Do you have a motto? Make it perfect.

MOVE QUICKLY, DIVE IN AND PUSH

Mike Tilly came to New Orleans from California to pursue ocean engineering when Louisiana was the leader in subsea engineering due to its work in oil and gas production. That inspired Mike's interest in the environment and ignited a move toward the recycling of technology and materials management with the launch of proForce in 2003.

What was your first job? Diving and subsea development for ODECO. Next was General Dynamics in undersea warfare.

Undersea warfare? Undersea robots and remotely operated vehicles that come out like a torpedo and then determine what to do out in the open ocean.

For what purpose? This was targeted toward the Russian submarine threat.

What made you go out on your own? I saw a niche in recycling electronics and started Technology Exchange, which is now proForce.

What do you do? Legislation requires companies with large amounts of capital assets to track them to death. We help companies keep tabs on them and help manage their surplus materials.

How do you make money? We get paid for taking a client's surplus assets, selling some of it and disposing of the rest in accordance with all regulations. We also take surplus materials, process them and resell them on eBay.

What did you do to accelerate your growth? Within the first year, we added investment recovery and materials management to our services. Because of the immense need for services after Hurricane Katrina, our business took off.

What was most challenging? Getting initial clients and projects, followed by the chaos of post-Karina.

How do you hope to create change? The electronics part of it is protecting the landfills and the environment from Mercury and toxic heavy metals in electronic waste (e-waste).

For something to work like this, how do you sell? It's a matter of coming up with projects that make sense to clients. We have to convince them that the services we provide are not only the right thing to do, but that they make sense economically.

What is your growth strategy? We have developed some unique storm recovery programs that are of interest to utilities along the Gulf Coast.

What challenges you the most? Personnel and managing people. Hiring and firing and getting the right mix are key to keeping everyone moving in the right direction.

What are the most important aspects of your operation? Sales and marketing are the keys to the company.

What inspires you? Developing something new and different and seeing people embrace it keeps me rolling.

Define excellence. It's an attitude.

What lessons have you learned? When you have an opportunity, move quickly, dive in and push.

What assets exist in New Orleans for early-stage companies? We have the universities, the entrepreneurs and the networks. We just need available money.

FOCUS ON QUALITY

Photographed by Rachel Dory

Brent McCrossen was a toddler when he realized his destiny was to be in the music industry. At 24 years old, he threw his drums and clothes in the back of his car and moved to Seattle without a job, friends or anyone to fix his traffic tickets. It was there, in 2005, that he came up with the idea for a new kind of music licensing agency, Audiosocket, which he ultimately brought back to New Orleans.

How did you get started in music? My grandfather, who was kind of a comedian, bought me a set of drums to get even with my parents. He kept giving me drums and knew I was destined to be a musician. Turns out he was right.

What does Audiosocket do? We are a music licensing agency. We take music from all over the world, New Orleans included, and secure the rights to represent it and place it in media.

What media? Film, TV, video games, commercial advertisements and retail broadcasts. We go anywhere that has media and an opportunity to play music.

How did you begin? I had lived in New Orleans my entire life and lacked a challenge. Moving to Seattle, I was not as fulfilled with the culture, so I decided to bring something to the city to anchor me there.

What was that? I brought big Mardi Gras parties to the city. They were raging events with sold out crowds, parades, second lines, bands, stuff they had never seen before. Because of this, bands started asking me to manage them, and venues started asking me to do their talent buying, so I started a company called Interface.

How did you make the jump to licensing? Some of my musicians were being used by major media outlets like the Sopranos and Activision video games. I realized that I could scale that and get content from all over world in a broad scope of musical styles. From there I started developing a business plan.

What made the plan a reality? I met Jen Anderson Miller, an extreme sports film developer who came to me for music. She had complaints about the tedious process and time required to license music. We knew there had to be a better way, so we talked about my idea. One night over margaritas, we decided to go for it.

How are you different? Our technology allows you to license a song in a matter of seconds rather than months, and our catalogue features only the best of the best from every genre.

Describe your early success. Our first deal with McDonald's was a national sweet tea commercial featuring a local hip-hop artist, MC Know One. The reward in all of this is when you can call an artist who is working his tail off, doing what he loves and say, "Hey, we just got you a five-figure deal and national exposure."

What's in your portfolio? There are about 25,000 songs in our catalogue and growing, but our focus is quality, not quantity. Some songs will move out as others move in because people are always looking for something fresh.

Why did you bring the company to New Orleans? The whole time I knew I wanted to bring the business here, especially with the budding film industry. Films were shooting and editing here but going back to Los Angeles for their music source.

Who are some of your clients? We've got deals with A&E, Toyota, McDonald's, Converse, Nickelodeon and MTV Networks, to name a few.

You knew you made it when? We inked a deal with MTV.

Your mantra? Failure is not an option.

TURN IT GREEN

Don Kelly is a lawyer who loved music so much that he decided to use it to raise money for charity. After a series of successful concerts, his young daughter questioned the recycling effort in New Orleans. Applying her logic to his love of music events, he launched Project 30-90 in September 2009, turning music festivals into sustainable events.

What do you hope to do? Produce events that are national in scope and talent while being sustainable and eco-friendly.

Where did 30-90 come from? The latitude and longitude of New Orleans.

How did you get your idea? While evacuated for Katrina, I wanted to do a benefit concert for kids' charities.

Had you ever produced a concert? No, I was just a fan.

What is your day job? A practicing lawyer.

How did you secure musicians? I cold-called them.

How did your first concert fare? It was the first post-Katrina concert where only iconic New Orleans musicians got together in the city and played – it was powerful.

What did it teach you? That I needed to do more to prepare than going to see music at Tipitina's.

Why did this turn into something green? My daughter's logic that recycling is good so everyone should do it was so simple that it made perfect sense. I just took it and applied it to my love of concert production. The idea of doing a large event on solar power seemed plausible to me, so off I went.

Your next steps? I researched and found a company that had done smaller stages on solar power, and I challenged them to join me in making a large-scale event possible.

Did you meet resistance? People were skeptical over whether an event like this could be done completely eco-friendly. We knew it was possible.

How did you produce the concert? We ran a main stage with seven bands, and we powered that stage, the lights and the sound completely on solar power.

Were you surprised it worked? Everyone has been blown away that we pulled it off.

What else became green? Paperless tickets and biodegradable serving supplies made out of corn and sugar. We recycled all of the plastic bottles and sold t-shirts made from recycled bottles.

Were there any other incentives? For an additional $2, we offered a green ticket offset for the ticket buyer to microfinance a carbon reduction project.

What did you learn that you wish you had known from the start? That marketing a project like this is very complex and time consuming.

What is your best advice? Learn everything that you can by volunteering. Then at some point you just have to take the leap.

What's next? We are already working to expand the concert into a two-day event.

Define excellence. Pursuing your dream with unbridled passion.

CHANGE THE LANDSCAPE

Robert LeBlanc created Lifestyle Revolution Group (LRG) to partner with real estate developers and create entertainment venues and restaurants in urban settings that celebrate entrepreneurship, fashion and art. The company was founded in late 2005, during the aftermath of Hurricane Katrina, to create a sense of community among the people intent on revitalizing New Orleans' business, artistic and philanthropic landscapes. He is positioned to be the Ralph Lauren of the entertainment industry.

So you run a group of clubs and spaces – what makes them different? We see ourselves as the connective tissue for entrepreneurs – a bit of a concierge, too. It's our job to personalize the city for established and newly-located businesses and to ingratiate them with the community.

Why did you start? We were born in post-Katrina New Orleans as an amalgamation of displaced employees and companies that wanted to create a sense of community for all those returning to and moving to New Orleans. We wanted to provide comfortable, creative venues for the change makers in the community to get together, relax and do good.

Who is your target market? 20-35 year olds.

What did you study? I'm a Math nerd – Economics and Finance.

How did you wind up in this business? My grandfather was the ultimate host.

What business strategy do you wish you had perfected from the start? Complete excellence in everything we do relative to our guests' experiences.

In business, what is your idea of perfect happiness? Changing the social and entertainment landscape in some really important, meaningful and positive way.

What is your greatest fear? Not pushing hard enough. Not going far enough.

How do you view failure? As an opportunity to learn what not to do next time.

Which kind of person can you live without? Those who have no concept of creating mutually beneficial relationships and value. They are the ones who believe that if they are not screwing someone else over, then they are getting screwed over.

What do you consider the most overrated virtue? Caution.

Which words or phrases do you most overuse? "My apologies," but they are always necessary because of all of the mistakes I make.

If you could change one thing about yourself, what would it be? I'd love to make at least one meeting on time.

Where's your business now? We're at $10 million in revenue with five entertainment venues in place. The sixth is in the works and should be complete by June 2010.

What's next? We're in negotiations with Baton Rouge developers to replicate what we've done in New Orleans. Doing the same with Louisville, Kentucky and, potentially, Washington, D.C.

And the future of LRG? I believe we can be a $100 - $150 million company in the next five to six years.

Your goal? To become what Ralph Lauren is to fashion in the entertainment industry – creating fine venues and classy experiences for people worldwide.

THINK BEFORE YOU BITE

From left: Randy Crochet, Jeff Leach, Brook Fillinger

Randy Crochet and Jeff Leach, a realtor and archeologist respectively, were an unlikely pair to open a healthy pizza joint. More a movement than a fast food shop, NAKEDpizza was formed in 2006 and looked at natural diets to create a pizza that breaks down food to its natural version. Now with partners Mark Cuban and the Kraft Group, NAKEDpizza will be rolling out all over the country.

What did you first name your business? World's Healthiest Pizza.

How did you do? It was difficult, the name was hard for people to swallow.

Did you start with a plan? Yes, and we have made every mistake you can make.

But you won Mark Cuban's national business plan contest. You must be doing something right. We wanted to show that pizza doesn't have to be part of the problem. In our national epidemic of chronic disease and obesity, pizza can even be part of the solution.

What have you done to pizza? We approached it from a food-science perspective and created a formula by combining biological and nutritional science. We "hacked" the business model.

So what is your secret? Our evolutionary perspective and creation of a "functional" fast food.

Why functional foods? Functional foods are a way forward. As for our pizza specifically, we provide a range of nutrients that restore balance and well-being.

Does it still taste good? Delicious.

What makes this work? Food is the biggest business in the world, and we will draft behind the big boys.

What is your mission? To use pizza as a tool to improve the health and well-being of our customers in a meaningful way and use that same pizza as a communication tool. A way to have a conversation.

Where do you see the pizza business 20 years from now? Right now, pizza is the unhealthiest fast food in the country. We are confident that all pizza will be eaten this way 20 years from now.

Was this the best place to launch a healthy pizza operation? If we make it in a city that doesn't pride itself on its health, we can make it anywhere.

What's next? Our equity partners are Mark Cuban, owner of the Dallas Mavericks, and the Kraft Group, the family that owns the Patriots. They will franchise throughout Texas and the New England area. We are entering into a large number of area development agreements to start NAKEDpizzas across the United States in 2010.

How will you expand? By awarding smart locations, not selling areas randomly, allowing for a tighter level of engagement and better percentage of success.

With so much interest, how do you choose franchisees? We are seeking individuals and groups who share our world view.

What's most challenging about your rapid growth? Managing the roll out and opening of multiple markets while finding good people.

Business motto? Think before you bite and livNAKED.

WORD OF MOUTH MARKETING

Suzanne Perron looks the part of a bridal designer: beautiful, soft-spoken, poised and focused on the details. After a stint as one of Vera Wang's top designers, she decided to head South in 2006 and set up shop in an old home on Magazine Street's historic six-mile shopping corridor.

When did you start sewing? At age five. My mother and grandmother both sewed. I started sewing skirts for myself in kindergarten, and from that point on, I wanted to be a designer. I still have the first skirt I ever made.

Who bought your first sewing machine? The Easter Bunny brought me a pink child's sewing machine from Sears. I was too determined to start sewing for my parents to wait for my birthday or Christmas.

When did you make sewing a business? I graduated from LSU in fashion before moving to New York to study at the Fashion Institute of Technology. I was hired out of school by Carolina Herrera. I went on to work in the fashion industry for over 13 years.

What did you do in New York? I worked on the design teams of several well-known designers. I was known and valued for my technical skills and knowledge of construction, draping and pattern making.

What is draping? The first three-dimensional interpretation of the garment. It is the art of manipulating blocks of fabric on the mannequin until what you have cut and pinned together looks like the designer's sketch.

Were you managing other people in the process? Yes. I managed a staff of cutters and sewers as well as assistants and student interns. I did not sew in New York - I had talented seamstresses sewing under my direction.

So you took designers' sketches and turned them into garments? Exactly. Now I take my sketches and turn them into garments.

Do you like any particular type of garment? I love specialty evening gowns. I am intrigued by the juxtaposition of hard and soft - the structured foundation on the inside and the soft outer fashion layer.

What other fashion designers did you work for? I went on to work for Anna Sui. Her work was rock-and-roll meets vintage. I later went back to couture by freelancing for Chado Ralph Rucci. My final design position in New York was with Vera Wang. There, I really grew in my craft and developed a greater passion for bridal and ball gowns.

What brought you to New Orleans? My mother and grandmother both grew up here, so this had always felt like home. No matter where we lived, holidays were in New Orleans. After 13 years away, I was ready to come home. Bringing my experiences back to New Orleans, I opened Suzanne Perron to create an opportunity to employ and develop local talent.

What matters most in business? Satisfied clients. The client is my priority.

What is your niche? Once in a lifetime gowns for brides and debutantes.

What is your process? Initial consultation, sketching, muslin fitting and final gown fitting.

What makes your clients happy? Seeing the gown of their dreams come to life and knowing that it was uniquely crafted just for them.

How do you market? Word of mouth. There's nothing like a beautiful bride walking down the aisle.

Kyle Berner was walking through a market in Thailand when he came across some flip-flops and immediately loved the comfort on his feet. Hoping to help people from the impoverished country, he approached the shoe supplier and discovered a quality product that was environmentally friendly. Founded in 2008, Feelgoodz, Berner's New Orleans-based business, now sells flip-flops internationally and is building a global brand based upon ethics, sustainability and comfort.

What initially brought you to Thailand? Adventure.

What makes this product stand out? The flip-flops are very comfortable, produced ethically and are made from natural rubber. Our story and social misson make us stand out as well.

How are the flops made? From midnight to 6 a.m., they tap on the tree with a tool to get the liquid rubber from the tree. After the liquid rubber hardens a bit, it is rolled into rubber sheets and non-toxic dyes are added. The sheets are then compressed with high heat, cut into flops, buffered for smooth edges, and the strap is placed in the flop. In Thailand, the tropical climate is perfect for natural rubber harvesting.

Is sustainability important? Very.

Avenue for import? By sea through Bangkok.

Who selects your colors? My mom and sisters are my chief fashion consultants.

How did you start? My partner and I formed the company in April 2008 (on his wedding day, in fact). Two months later, our first shipment of 300 pairs arrived. We sold out in two weeks and knew we were onto something.

What tough questions have you faced from discerning customers? Do your flip-flops biodegrade on my feet while I wear them?

What challenges you? Managing cash flow both in and out. But at the same time, it's fun bootstrapping it.

Have you met your product demand capacity? We have a hard time meeting demand, but that's a great problem to have.

Are you still the lead salesperson? I am, but we also have a team in Hawaii and Canada.

Besides Whole Foods, where are your other top markets? The natural product market is our main focus, but there's also the collegiate, surf, spa, yoga, kids and eco-boutiques. I could keep going...

Is there anything you have learned that you wish you had known from the start? You can never plan too early. The plan will rarely, if ever, go according to plan, and you have to stay fluid, but it certainly gives you guidance.

Do you envision an expanded product line? Absolutely! We've tossed around ideas such as yoga mats, mattresses, t-shirts, hammocks and ping-pong paddles. But however we expand, it must fall under the ethos of "Green, Comfortable, Ethical."

Was this your first job? Not at all. I've been a banquet waiter, a basketball coach, a computer salesperson and a hot dog cart vendor. Again, I could go on and on!

Are there other entrepreneurs in this space? Yes, there are. But none with a business model, marketing model and social model like ours.

Are flip-flops a fad? Not at all.

Do you prefer grass or pavement? Grass. Easy.

CHANGE THE GAME

Nic Perkin left the London Business School never dreaming he would one day wind up in New Orleans running one of the fastest growing companies in the state. The Receivables Exchange, founded in 2007, allows businesses to sell their receivables to a global network of institutional investors and access working capital in as little as three days.

How does your company work? We have an electronic exchange model similar to eBay. Businesses can generate cash quickly by selling short-term debt at auction. Buyers, on the other side, earn a profit when retailers or others pay the debt back.

Who are sample sellers? We have sellers from 37 industries, including manufacturing, media and technology.

And the buyers? Institutional buyers, hedge funds, banks and others.

You are experiencing tremendous growth – to what do you owe that? By manufacturing ideas and innovation in this space. We are creating the market.

What is the most important tool to master for a start up? Selling.

Where were you trained? I worked at Bear Stearns, which is the best cold-call training you could ever receive.

Going back to your younger years, what was your first job? I had a dog walking business in eighth grade. It grew so much that I hired my friends.

Did you always like business? As a child, I was required to read the *Wall Street Journal* every day.

What is your background? I was Executive Vice President at EmSense Corporation, a next generation media measurement company, and then was Vice President of Global Business Development for Massive, Inc., which was acquired by Microsoft Corporation in 2006.

Was Massive innovative? Massive was a leading network for dynamic video game advertising.

Before that you worked on Wall Street? Yes, as head of Strategic Business Development at Kestrel Technologies, a leading Wall Street developer of technology solutions for fixed income trading. I did M&A and held various operations positions at The Black Book. I also saw the mini crash in 1989.

What did the market teach you? There are no shortcuts.

Why did you decide to come to New Orleans to start Receivables Exchange? I analyzed the marketplace for two years and found that the commercial code of Louisiana allowed a company to make money at this.

What is your business philosophy? If you are not game changing, you are not getting funded.

What do you wish you had known from the start? I wish I had better understood the anatomy of the word "No." If you are changing the marketplace, almost everything starts with people telling you no.

Does operating from New Orleans help or hurt? It helps because we are now the iconic city of reinvention and our company is reinventing an industry.

Best advice? You are only responsible for your own behavior. Stick to your principles.

What motivates you? The worst phrase in the English language: "Because that's the way it's always been done."

DREAM BIG, PLAY HARD

Lavonzell Nicholson is launching a new sports league in New Orleans, one that has the entrepreneurial community abuzz. PlayNOLA began in 2009 and hopes to create a premier sports and social club, bringing new teams to fields and gyms across the region.

What do you do? We provide hundreds of New Orleanians the opportunity to not only be physically active but also to build unique social and professional relationships in a safe and enjoyable environment.

Why here? We want to use the green space in New Orleans to bridge imaginary boundaries. This is a moment in time that we want look back on and know that we were able to impact the city.

Where else do leagues like this take place? Chicago, Nashville, Austin, Las Vegas and San Diego.

Why sports? Sports provide a neutral zone that allows people of all ages to connect.

What type of sports will be played? Flag football, dodge ball and basketball in the fall. In the spring, softball, kickball, sailing, soccer and ultimate Frisbee.

How many people can play? Over 1,500 the first year.

What keeps you up at night? The start-up phase of a business is always changing, so I have had to change with it and lose some "linear" thinking.

What is most challenging? The challenge has been starting a business in a very public way. We won the 504ward business plan competition, so there is the pressure to be successful and the pressure of meeting many different expectations.

What is your greatest asset? We have assembled an awesome team who will collectively push an overall quality of life.

When are you most creative? When I am working with the team. The ability to bounce ideas off each other, gather thoughts and different opinions is the best way to work!

What are you learning about yourself while building the company? I am pushing myself in ways that I would have never imagined. The energy and passion for my business keeps me moving.

How do you define excellence? Maintaining your integrity and honoring your word. I think that goes a very long way.

What formal training, if any, do you wish you had that you don't? I don't know if there is any formal training that could have prepared me for this journey. Life lessons from work experiences, formal education, success and failures have taken me to this moment.

What is hard about being an entrepreneur? It pushes you to the edge in a way that others looking from the outside just don't understand. You have moments of confidence and elation, then moments of anxiety and fear.

What does it really mean to be successful? That I enjoy what I am doing and people who are engaged enjoy it as well. Not just the first time but every time.

What did you learn from the greatest failure of your life? When one door closes, there is another one opening. It is up to you to decide whether you walk through it. We all make the wrong decision once, or maybe even twice, but we have to keep moving.

Lessons learned? Everyone won't see your vision and that's okay. You may have to paint the picture for them. Work is hard and may even get harder.

What is your motto? Dream big. Don't have it any other way, you will only cheat yourself in the end.

CREATE A DIFFERENT CHANNEL

Jeff Berger was a student at Tulane University when he began to analyze commercial uses of social networking. Hatching the idea to marry social networking with help in finding a job, Berger launched KODA in 2009, which has already gained national attention and is now in its initial product launch.

How did you begin? My partner Tony York and I were looking around at ventures targeting the college demographic.

You both had the entrepreneurial itch? Our first venture was a tool to make the college move-in process easier by bringing retailers into one online marketplace.

What happened? The venture failed, but we knew we were onto something.

What next? We held a brainstorming session with web developers from Silicon Valley. Our objective was to service the college demographic. The job market was a natural arena since jobs are essential and there was no great place for young talent to find a job.

What did your analysis show? That job sites were not targeting our demographic, that social networking wasn't helping anyone find a job and that career centers are limited in the help that they can provide.

What does KODA do? We are a place for professional identity. Rather than deciding from a single-page resume, why not see their profile as a person and a more encompassing picture of who they are?

How is the product innovative? This is the first recruiting tool that brings the success of social networking to the job market.

What does a user do? He or she can create a professional profile using audio, video, text, attachments and the like to capture the user's professional and intellectual attributes.

Why does the market need this? Because a social tool provides so much more flexibility than a regular "job" tool for both the employer and prospective employee.

Is it just for individuals? No, we have hundreds of companies that have joined to post their profiles and job opportunities.

And these companies are interested in younger workers? Exactly.

Are your services free? Yes.

How do you market? On college campuses, social networking websites, to databases of our target market and through blogs.

How can bloggers help? Organic marketing is very powerful for a tool like this.

What is the benefit to young people? Jobs. People start using KODA in high school and college. The site encourages them to add their different and interesting activities and accomplishments through the years. This larger picture showcasing the individual is what a potential employer will see to determine if they want to hire this person.

What has you the most excited? It's thrilling to watch your product come to life and to see people you don't know using the site.

What challenges you the most? There's no formal education on how to handle bugs.

What is your goal? To create an opportunity website and a different channel for people to think about education.

FURTHER INFORMATION

What Becomes a Legend

Edmund McIlhenny, McIlhenny Company, established 1868 (www.tabasco.com)

George Leidenheimer, Leidenheimer Bakery, established 1896 (www.leidenheimer.com)

Sam Zemurray, United Fruit Company, established 1899 (www.unitedfruit.org)

William B. Reily, Reily Foods Company, established 1902 (www.reilyfoods.com)

Dr. George Tichenor, Dr. G.H. Tichenor Antiseptic Company, established 1905 (www.drtichenor.com)

Sydney Besthoff, K&B (Katz and Besthoff), established 1905

Arthur and Henry Boh, Boh Bros Construction, established 1909 (www.bohbros.com)

William Burkenroad, Green Coffee Association, established 1923

Sam Pulitzer, Wembley Inc., established 1926

Joseph Jones, Canal Barge Company, established 1933 (www.canalbarge.com)

Pierre Bagur, Aunt Sally's Candy Shop, established 1935 (www.auntsallys.com)

Andrew J. Higgins, Higgins Industries, established 1938

James Viavant, Avondale Marine Ways, Inc., established 1938

Dr. Alton Ochsner, Ochsner Health System, established 1942 (www.ochsner.org)

Stephen Goldring, Magnolia Liquor Company, established 1944

Donald Bollinger, Bollinger Shipyards, established 1946 (www.bollingershipyards.com)

Owen Edward Brennan, Brennan's Restaurant, established 1946 (www.brennansneworleans.com)

Niels F. Johnsen, International Shipholding, established 1947 (www.intship.com)

James Martial "J.M." Lapeyre, Laitram L.L.C, established 1949 (www.laitrammachinery.com)

Robert L. Suggs, Petroleum Helicopters, Inc., established 1949 (www.phihelico.com)

Ruth Fertel, Ruth's Chris Steak House, established 1965 (www.ruthschris.com)

Patrick F. Taylor, Taylor Energy Company, established 1979 (www.taylorenergy.com)

Al Copeland, Al Copeland Investments, established 1983 (www.alcopeland.com)

At The Helm

Jerry Goldman, Friede & Goldman, established 1946 (www.fng.com)

Cosimo Matassa, J&M Recording Studio, established 1945

Leah Chase, Dooky Chase, established 1946

Alden "Doc" Laborde, Ocean Drilling and Exploration Company, established 1953

Blaine Kern, Kern Productions, established 1947 (www.mardigrasproductions.com)

John Laborde, Tidewater Marine, established 1956 (www.tdw.com)

Ted Kritikos, Owensby and Kritikos, established 1962 (www.ok-insp.com)

David Oreck, Oreck Corporation, established 1963 (www.oreck.com)

Peter Mayer, Peter A. Mayer Advertising, Inc., established 1967 (www.peteramayer.com)

Tom Benson, New Orleans Saints, established 1967 (www.neworleanssaints.com)

James R. "Jim Bob" Moffett, McMoRan Exploration Company, established 1969 (www.mcmoran.com)

Mignon Faget, Mignon Faget, established 1969 (www.mignonfaget.com)

Quint Davis, Festival Productions, Inc., established 1970 (www.fpi-no.com)

Alton Doody, Alton F. Doody Company, established 1972

Darryl Berger, The Berger Company, established 1972 (www.darrylberger.com)

Prentiss "P.C." Havens, Seismic Exchange, Inc., established 1975 (www.seismicexchange.com)

Paul Prudhomme, Chef Paul Prudhomme, established 1979 (www.kpauls.com)

Phyllis Jordan, PJ's Coffee of New Orleans, established 1978 (www.pjscoffee.com)

David Guidry, Guico Machine Works, established 1982 (www.guicoindustries.com)

Bobby Savoie, Science and Engineering Associates, established 1986 (www.geocent.com)

George Shinn, New Orleans Hornets, established 1987 (www.nba.com/hornets)

Victor Castellon, Castellon Pharmacies, established 1988

John E. Koerner, Koerner Capital, established 1995

Roger Ogden, Roger H. Ogden Development, established 1995 (www.rogerogden.com)

Rich Ashman, Charter Research Inc., established 2003

On The Horizon

Jimmy Treuting, Communiqué, Inc., established 1992 (www.communique.com)

Joel Dondis, Joel Catering and Events, established 1993 (www.joels.com)

Harold Clarke, Harold Clarke Haute Couture, established 1994 (www.haroldclarke.com)

Todd Hornbeck, Hornbeck Offshore Services, established 1997 (www.hornbeckoffshore.com)

Mark Samuels, Basin Street Records, established 1997 (www.basinstreetrecords.com)

Jonathan Ferrara, Jonathan Ferrara Gallery, established 1998 (www.jonathanferraragallery.com)

Kenneth Purcell, iSeatz, established 1999 (www.iseatz.com)

Matt Wisdom, TurboSquid, established 2000 (www.turbosquid.com)

Ron Markham & Irvin Mayfield, New Orleans Jazz Orchestra, established 2002 (www.thenojo.com)

Arnold Baker, Baker Ready Mix, established 2003 (www.bakerreadymix.com)

Chris Schultz, Voodoo Ventures, established 2003 (www.voodooventures.com)

Jon Sherman, Flavor Paper, established 2003 (www.flavoleague.com)

Mike Tilly, proForce, established 2003 (www.proforceus.com)

Brent McCrossen, Audiosocket, established 2005 (www.audiosocketmusic.com)

Don Kelly, Don Kelly Productions, established 2005 (www.donkellyproductions.com)

Robert LeBlanc, Lifestyle Revolution Group, established 2005 (www.lrgnola.com)

Randy Crochet & Jeff Leach, NAKEDpizza, established 2006 (www.nakedpizza.biz)

Suzanne Perron, Suzanne Perron, established 2006 (www.suzanneperron.com)

Kyle Berner, Feelgoodz, established 2007 (www.feelgoodz.com)

Nic Perkin, Receivables Exchange, established 2007 (www.receivablesxchange.com)

Lavonzell Nicholson, playNOLA, established 2009 (www.playnola.com)

Jeff Berger, KODA, established 2009 (www.koda.us)

ACKNOWLEDGEMENTS

The entrepreneurs listed in these pages cover a broad range of industries over a wide span of time. Not only should we thank them, but also the people who supported them along the way and, through that, contributed greatly to our city. Many of the descendants of the deceased entrepreneurs spent significant time helping me to research and understand their family members' early business development.

We would like to thank James Nolan, whose guidance in design and editing made this book come to life. Lauren Baum and Nicky Henriquez from The Idea Village offered constant supervision and support. Betsy Ellis and Cameron Yancey worked tirelessly on every detail. Alex Faust, Kathryn Isenmann, Jeff Sandman, Beau Thomas and the rest of The Idea Village team also lent tremendous support to the project. Thank you to the Darkroom, an instrumental partner in the photographic production of this book. Ron, Cassidy, McClain, Ken, Kingsley and Megan all earn a gold star for their love as we toiled away. An additional thanks to Dan, Cat, our parents and all of our supportive friends.

For their fearless leadership and endless support, The Idea Village would like to thank its past and present Board of Directors and Advisors, Tiffany Adler, Taylor Beery, Darryl d'Aquin, Quentin Dastugue, Alton Doody, Allen Eskew, Carla Fishman, Sam Giberga, Mason Granger, David Guidry, James Hardy, Bill Hines, Leslie Jacobs, Scott Jacobs, Yvette Jones, Merritt Lane, Alden McDonald, Suzanne Mestayer, John Payne, Steve Perry, Mark Romig, Tim Ryan, David Sylvester, Jimmy Treuting, Robbie Vitrano, Rod West and Matthew Wisdom. Specifically, we thank our Chairman, Mark Romig, and inaugural Chairman, Merritt Lane, who offered invaluable guidance and direction in producing the book.

Also important to acknowledge is the community of believers who have supported developing an entrepreneurial community, including Blue Moon Foundation, City of New Orleans, United States Department of Commerce, Fox Family Foundation, Entergy Charitable Foundation, HCA Delta Divison, Rosenthal & Jacobs Foundation, Jones Family Foundation, Jones Walker, JP Morgan Chase, Louisiana Disaster Recovery Foundation, Louisiana Recovery Authority, New Orleans Business Council, Regions Bank, Rockefeller Foundation, RosaMary Foundation, State of Louisiana, Trumpet Group, Tulane University and University of New Orleans.

Special thanks to Charlotte Gottesman, who generously commissioned The Idea Village to produce this book, which was also made possible by the belief of Lee Adler, Linda and Neil Baum, Ann and Bill Bell, LouEllen and Darryl Berger, Cathy and Rivie Cary, Bonnie and William Conway, Bill Goldring, Lisa and Sandy Gottesman, Beth James, Elly Lane, Mary Lucy and David Lane, Diana and Tom Lewis, Sean Levine, Amanda Majkowski, Mark Mayer, Suzanne and Michael Mestayer, Linda and Michael Miller, Carolyn Mitchell, Michelle Oakes, Kevin Pollard, Marcia and Bill Rafkin, Debbie and Rick Rees, Jane and Bill Sizeler, Chris Skinner, Susu and Andrew Stall, Melba and Moise Steeg, Rob Stumm, Mike Tilly and Sarah and Tommy Usdin. What started as a small book has grown into the first-ever documentation of the history of entrepreneurship in New Orleans.

Finally, we'd like to thank the founders of The Idea Village, especially the inspiration and passion of Allen Bell, Sam Giberga, Darin McAuliffe, Michele Reynoir, Robbie Vitrano and Tim Williamson for their belief in the potential of rare individuals who are crazy enough to believe they can change the world.